THE REBELLION:

UNDERSTANDING SATAN'S CHARACTER, MOTIVES, AND LAST-DAY DECEPTIONS

A Devotional-__________ Guide for Navigating the Great Controversy in Modern Life

Advent Awareness
PUBLISHING & MEDIA

MICHAEL A. REAHL

Dedication

To every believer serving in uniform, in hospitals, and in homes, you are already commissioned. May your life be a living testimony of God's presence in the field where He has placed you.

TABLE OF CONTENTS

Preface

Writing has always helped me understand the truth more deeply. Throughout my life I have found joy in studying, researching, teaching, and sharing what I learn with others. Whether through conversations with friends, guiding people in moments of crisis, or writing on my blog, I have consistently been drawn to explaining the great themes of Scripture and the character of God. Putting these reflections into written form has not only shaped my own spiritual growth, but has also become a way to offer something meaningful to anyone seeking a clearer picture of truth.

My background in the military, emergency medicine, law enforcement, public health, and biblical studies has shaped how I see the world and how I understand the spiritual conflict unfolding around us. From the discipline of Army life to the pressure of emergency response to the rigorous study of Scripture in graduate school, each chapter of my experience has impressed upon me that we are living in a far larger conflict than we often recognize. The great controversy between Christ and Satan is not merely a theological framework. It is the story behind every struggle, every temptation, and every decision that forms our character.

This book represents my effort to bring together careful biblical study, theological reflection, and practical insight into the themes of Lucifer's fall, his accusations, and his ongoing influence in the world today. I write for readers who seek clarity in a time of confusion, for pastors and teachers desiring a dependable theological resource, and for believers navigating a digital culture that constantly shapes identity, attention, and purpose. My hope is that these chapters deepen your understanding of God's character and strengthen your confidence in His goodness.

Above all, I pray that these pages draw your attention to the love of God revealed in Jesus Christ. The great controversy is not a story of fear but of a God who grants freedom, answers deception with truth, and restores the human mind and heart through His grace. If these words help you trust Him more fully and see His character more clearly, then the purpose of this book has been fulfilled.

As you move through these chapters, you will notice a deliberate progression. The early sections lay the biblical foundation for understanding Lucifer's character, motives, and the origins of the great controversy. From there, the narrative follows the unfolding of the conflict throughout Scripture, culminating in Christ's ministry and His decisive victory at the cross. Later chapters examine Satan's strategies in the modern world, including the pressures of identity, distraction, and digital influence. My hope is that this structure guides you step by step from the beginning of the controversy to its final resolution, and that each chapter strengthens your confidence in the faithfulness of God.

Note to Reader

As you begin this book, I want to share something that will help you understand the way the chapters are written and the tools I use along the way. During my studies at Liberty University, I spent time learning biblical Greek and Hebrew. I learned how to work with resources such as Bible Hub or Bible.cc, lexicons, interlinear, and basic exegetical guides. These tools helped me study Scripture more carefully and understand the meaning of key words in ways that enrich and clarify the message of the Bible.

I want to be clear that I am not writing as a professional linguist or as an expert in ancient languages. I am writing as a responsible student of Scripture who loves to study and who wants to share what I have learned in a way that is simple and helpful. My goal is accuracy and clarity, not complexity.

From time to time you will see a Greek or Hebrew word in these chapters. I include these words only when they add something meaningful. Sometimes the original language highlights a shade of meaning that gets lost in translation. Sometimes it helps remove a misunderstanding. Sometimes it deepens the theological point that the passage is making. Whenever I reference an original word, I explain it in everyday language. There will be no complex grammar and no academic overload. Everything is kept simple, clear, and tied directly to the biblical text itself.

You do not need any prior knowledge of Hebrew or Greek to read this book. You do not need to be familiar with language tools or advanced study resources. Scripture is trustworthy in every translation, and God speaks through His Word with clarity and power. The original languages simply help illuminate certain ideas when appropriate.

If you ever want to explore a word more deeply, you are welcome to use free and easy resources such as Bible Hub or Bible.cc. They place strong study tools right at your fingertips, even if you have never taken a language class. But these tools are optional. You can read this book with confidence without using anything more than your Bible.

I write these things with humility. I am a fellow student of Scripture who is still learning, still growing, and still seeking to understand God's Word more faithfully. My desire is not to impress you with knowledge but to draw your attention to Christ and to the truth that sets us free. If the explanations in these pages help you see God's character more clearly, then they have fulfilled their purpose.

May God bless you as you read, study, and grow in His grace.

PART I

THE ORIGIN OF THE CONTROVERSY

CHAPTER ONE

The Beautiful Beginning

Before the mystery of sin entered the universe, before rebellion fractured the perfect harmony of heaven, Scripture reveals a creation filled with joy, order, and radiant peace. The government of God rested upon the unchanging foundation of His character. His law expressed His love, His authority flowed from His goodness, and every created being reflected the beauty of His wisdom and design. Heaven was a place of unity in purpose and affection, where every heart found delight in the presence of God.

Lucifer's Original Position and Nature

At the center of this harmony stood a being of remarkable brilliance and dignity. The prophet Ezekiel identifies him as the "anointed guardian cherub" placed by God upon His holy mountain (Ezekiel 28:14, ESV). The Hebrew word בורכ (keruv) refers to a heavenly being of exalted rank, entrusted with both proximity to God and responsibility before the universe.[1] Lucifer's position near

---

[1] Francis Brown, S. R. Driver, and Charles A. Briggs, *The Brown-Driver-Briggs Hebrew and English Lexicon* (Peabody, MA: Hendrickson, 1996), 500–501;

Ludwig Koehler, Walter Baumgartner, and Johann Jakob Stamm, *The Hebrew and Aramaic Lexicon of the Old Testament*, 2 vols. (Leiden: Brill, 1994–2000), 500.

"Keruv" refers to a high angelic being, often associated with divine presence, guardianship, and proximity to the throne of God.

the throne was not accidental. God placed him where His character could be understood most clearly and His glory reflected most beautifully.

Ezekiel also describes Lucifer as being created "blameless" in his ways. The Hebrew word תֹּם (tom)[2] carries the meaning of completeness, moral soundness, and full integrity (Ezekiel 28:15). Lucifer was crafted with a flawless character, pure intentions, and a mind capable of grasping profound truths about the nature of God. His wisdom was described as perfect, his appearance as breathtaking.[3] Scripture lists precious stones that adorned him, radiating beauty as they reflected the light surrounding the throne of God (Ezekiel 28:13). His glory was not his own. It was a gift bestowed by the Creator.

Ellen G. White affirms this picture of Lucifer's original dignity. She writes, "Lucifer was the covering cherub, holy and undefiled."[4] As one who stood in the very presence of God, he was honored above all created beings and entrusted with responsibilities that revealed both his

---

[2] BDB, 1070; HALOT, 1696. "Tom" denotes completeness, integrity, innocence, or blamelessness, often describing moral purity or wholeness.

[3] HALOT, 1696. The term 'perfect' (תמים, tamim) used elsewhere in Scripture reflects moral and functional completeness.

[4] Ellen G. White, *Patriarchs and Prophets* (Oakland, CA: Pacific Press, 1890), 35.

capacity and his Creator's confidence in him. Before sin, there was no hint of pride, rebellion, or dissatisfaction in him. Heaven recognized his gifts as tokens of divine love.

Harmony Before the Fall

Creation itself testified that God's government was grounded in freedom, trust, and love. Scripture consistently presents God's rule not as coercive but as the outflow of His perfect character. The psalmist declares, "Righteousness and justice are the foundation of Your throne; steadfast love and faithfulness go before You" (Psalm 89:14, ESV).[5] Throughout the Old Testament, God's authority is described in relational and moral terms, never arbitrary or authoritarian (Deuteronomy 32:4; Psalm 145:17). Even Jesus affirms the same divine reality when He teaches that God's law hangs on love (Matthew 22:37–40). In heaven, as on earth, obedience was the joyful response of beings who delighted in the goodness of their Creator.

The biblical witness supports this picture of heavenly harmony. Before the rebellion, the angels are portrayed

---

[5] Francis Brown, S. R. Driver, and Charles A. Briggs, *The Brown Driver Briggs Hebrew and English Lexicon* (Peabody, MA: Hendrickson, 1996), 841–842, s.v. "קֶדֶץ"; 1047–1048, s.v. "שָׁפְשִׂמ."

as a unified host, singing for joy at the creation (Job 38:7), ministering gladly before God (Psalm 103:20–21), and delighting to do His will.[6] Nothing in Scripture suggests that God demanded loyalty by force. Instead, His authority rested upon the transparency of His character and the free affection of His creatures.

Christian theologians across centuries echo this understanding. Augustine wrote that the blessedness of angels consisted in "cleaving to God with perfect obedience and enjoying Him."[7] Thomas Aquinas likewise argued that angelic joy flowed from the beatific vision, for "the angelic nature finds its beatitude in the vision of God."[8] John Calvin described angels as "ministers of His goodness" whose obedience was grounded in love, not constraint.[9] From the early church onward, Christians saw the harmony of heaven as the natural result of creatures oriented toward God in love.

Lucifer lived within this radiant fellowship. His identity was rooted in the God who created him "perfect in

[6] John N. Oswalt, *The Book of Isaiah: Chapters 1–39* (Grand Rapids, MI: Eerdmans, 1986), 304.

[7] Augustine, *The City of God*, trans. Henry Bettenson (London: Penguin, 2003), 11.9–12.

[8] Thomas Aquinas, *Summa Theologica*, I.62.

[9] John Calvin, *Institutes of the Christian Religion*, trans. Henry Beveridge (Peabody, MA: Hendrickson, 2008), 1.14.

wisdom and beauty" (Ezekiel 28:12–15). His purpose was tied to service, for angels were created as "ministering spirits" (Hebrews 1:14). His joy was complete in reflecting the character of the One who had given him life, for true joy exists only "in Your presence" (Psalm 16:11). Ellen G. White describes heaven before the fall as a realm where "every being found its highest happiness in the glory of God and the good of others."[10] This unity was not manufactured. It was the natural expression of lives aligned with divine love.

Adventist pioneers reinforced this biblical picture. Uriah Smith emphasized that obedience in heaven flowed from "voluntary, intelligent loyalty," not compulsion.[11] J. N. Andrews described the pre-fall universe as one governed by moral freedom, where each being served "from love and from the clear perception of God's goodness."[12] Theologians such as Ángel Manuel Rodríguez and Norman Gulley affirm the same: God governs through love,

---

[10] Ellen G. White, *The Great Controversy* (Mountain View, CA: Pacific Press, 1911), 493.

[11] Uriah Smith, *Thoughts on Daniel and the Revelation* (Battle Creek, MI: Review and Herald, 1897), 430.

[12] J. N. Andrews, "The Origin of Evil," *Review and Herald*, January 14, 1873, 52.

and harmony exists where His character is rightly understood.[13][14]

Thus, long before sin entered the universe, heaven operated on a principle radically different from the power structures of earth. The angels served because they loved. They obeyed because they trusted. Their unity flowed not from hierarchy alone but from hearts fully oriented toward the One who is love (1 John 4:8). In such an environment, rebellion was unthinkable until Lucifer shifted his gaze from God to self.

The Beauty That Magnifies the Tragedy

The beautiful beginning is essential for understanding the tragedy that follows. Evil did not arise because of a defect in God's creation. There was no flaw in the divine law. There was no injustice in God's throne. Sin originated in a perfect universe, in the heart of a being who had received the highest honor God could bestow. Uriah Smith notes that Lucifer stood in "an exalted position" and enjoyed "immense privilege and honor," yet he be-

---

[13] Ángel Manuel Rodríguez, *Message, Mission, and Unity of the Church* (Silver Spring, MD: Biblical Research Institute, 2013), 44;

[14] Norman R. Gulley, "The Cosmic Controversy: World View for Theology and Life," *Journal of the Adventist Theological Society* 7, no. 1 (1996): 88–90.

came "the first to forget the principles of God's government."[15] His fall was self-chosen, not divinely imposed.

Lucifer's original glory also reveals the depth of God's generosity. He held nothing back in creating this being. Lucifer's beauty, intelligence, and influence were expressions of divine love. None of these gifts suggested inequality, unfairness, or divine favoritism. Instead, they testified to the joy God takes in giving.

There was no reason for rebellion to begin. No pressure, no neglect, no limitation of freedom. Lucifer's story teaches us that the most dangerous form of sin is not born of hardship or deprivation, but of misplaced admiration, inward distortion, and self-focus. Before pride rose in his heart, Lucifer knew only the joy of service. Before envy touched him, he lived in the light of unbroken fellowship. Before self took the throne, he delighted in the glory of God.

The Foundation for the Great Controversy

This chapter lays the foundation for everything that follows. To understand the nature of Lucifer's fall, the psychology of sin, the disruption of heaven's harmony, and the accusations he later brought against God, we must

---

[15] Uriah Smith, *Thoughts on Daniel and the Revelation* (Battle Creek, MI: Review and Herald, 1882), commentary on Revelation 12.

begin with the truth that God created a perfect universe. There was no flaw in the divine character, no defect in divine love, and no restriction of creaturely freedom. The great controversy begins with the revelation of who God is and what He made.

The Shift Toward Rebellion

The transition from beauty to rebellion is not the story of a Creator who failed, but of a creature who turned away from the very source of his joy. As Chapter 2 will show, pride did not erupt suddenly. It grew subtly within a perfect environment, drawing the heart of Lucifer away from the One who created him and toward an identity shaped by self rather than God.

The beautiful beginning magnifies the tragedy of what Lucifer became, but it also magnifies the goodness of the God who made him. The more clearly we see the glory of heaven before the fall, the more fully we understand the justice, mercy, and love that underlie the entire story of the great controversy.

CHAPTER TWO

The Seeds of Pride

The fall of Lucifer did not begin with open rebellion or deliberate hostility toward God. Scripture shows that sin first appeared as a subtle change within the heart, a movement so quiet and imperceptible that only God could see its earliest form. The prophet Ezekiel describes this internal shift with striking simplicity: "Your heart was proud because of your beauty" (Ezekiel 28:17, ESV). The Hebrew verb הבג (gavah) means to rise, to lift oneself, or to become exalted in one's own estimation.[16] It does not refer to outward action at first, but to an internal elevation of self, a reshaping of identity from God-centered to self-centered. Pride began as a seed.

Lucifer's mind, which had once reflected the humility and joy of service, gradually turned inward. His gifts, originally recognized as expressions of divine love, became the source of self-admiration. The Hebrew word בל (lev), meaning heart, represents the center of thought,

---

[16] Francis Brown, S. R. Driver, and Charles A. Briggs, *The Brown-Driver-Briggs Hebrew and English Lexicon* (Peabody, MA: Hendrickson, 1996), 147;

Ludwig Koehler, Walter Baumgartner, and Johann Jakob Stamm, *The Hebrew and Aramaic Lexicon of the Old Testament*, 2 vols. (Leiden: Brill, 1994–2000), 172–173.

"Gavah" carries the nuance of being high, lifted up, or exalted, often referring to arrogance, pride, or elevation of self.

intention, and decision making.[17] Lucifer's heart began to turn away from trust in the Creator toward trust in himself. He no longer saw his beauty as a gift but as a possession. What God had given freely, Lucifer began to claim as personal entitlement.

This inward turn is the beginning of all sin. Ellen G. White describes this transformation vividly: "Little by little, Lucifer came to indulge a desire for self-exaltation. The high honors he received were not appreciated as the gift of God. He resented the position that Christ held by the appointment of the Father."[18] Pride did not erupt suddenly. It grew quietly. It was nourished in the soil of self-reflection, self-admiration, and self-dependence.

The prophet Isaiah exposes the internal dialogue that marked the birth of sin. Lucifer said in his heart, "I will ascend to heaven… I will make myself like the Most High" (Isaiah 14:13 to 14, ESV). The Hebrew phrase הלעא (eʾeleh), "I will ascend," conveys deliberate intention, an upward grasping motivated by ambition. The repeated use of "I will" reveals the shift from worship

---

[17] HALOT, 514–516; BDB, 524–525. "Lev" (heart) denotes the inner person, including intellect, will, motives, and moral character—especially in anthropological and theological contexts.

[18] Ellen G. White, *The Great Controversy* (Mountain View, CA: Pacific Press, 1911), 494.

to aspiration, from receiving God's glory to seeking his own. Pride was not merely a feeling. It became a chosen direction of thought. Lucifer desired position rather than purpose, authority rather than service, and independence rather than trust.

The early Adventist pioneers understood this internal corruption. James White observed that Lucifer's fall began "when he permitted the admiration of himself to eclipse his admiration of the character of God."[19] J. N. Andrews similarly wrote that pride "perverted his wisdom and corrupted his loyalty," reminding us that sin does not require external temptation.[20] It can grow in the mind by changing how we see ourselves and how we view God.

The Hebrew term לָלַח (chalal), often translated as "profane" or "corrupt," carries the nuance of piercing or breaking something that was whole.[21] In Ezekiel 28:16, Lucifer "profane[d]" his sanctuaries, which suggests that what was pure and set apart for God became twisted by inward self-focus. The corruption of Lucifer's character

---

[19] James White, *Review and Herald*, January 9, 1855.

[20] J. N. Andrews, *The Thoughts of God Toward Man* (Battle Creek, MI: Review and Herald, 1865), 27.

[21] HALOT, 319–321; BDB, 320–322. "Chalal" includes meanings such as to profane, defile, pierce, violate, or make something common that was holy—indicating the breaking of sacred wholeness.

was not the destruction of his gifts but the distortion of them. His wisdom did not disappear; it was redirected. His influence did not fade; it was misused. His beauty did not diminish; it became the object of pride.

Ellen White writes that Lucifer "allowed his envy of Christ to prevail, and he became rebellious."[22] This phrase reveals an important truth: pride always reshapes relationships. Lucifer's desire for self-advancement created jealousy toward Christ, distrust toward God, and suspicion toward the very government he once supported. Pride does not stay internal. It begins inward, grows into comparison, matures into dissatisfaction, and ultimately produces open rebellion.

The apostle Paul warns believers that pride leads to the same spiritual downfall in human hearts. He cautions that a new believer must not be placed into leadership quickly, "or he may become puffed up with conceit" (τυφωθείς, typhotheis),[23] "and fall into the condemnation of the devil" (1 Timothy 3:6, ESV). The Greek verb τυφόω (tyfoo) means to be enveloped in smoke or blind-

---

[22] Ellen G. White, *Patriarchs and Prophets* (Oakland, CA: Pacific Press, 1890), 36.

[23] BDAG, 1030. τυφόω means 'to be conceited, blinded by pride,' derived from a root meaning 'to be enveloped in smoke,' conveying the image of moral or intellectual clouding.

ed by conceit. Pride obscures reality. It blinds the heart to truth. It makes a person unable to see God clearly or see themselves accurately. This blindness is part of Satan's own fall and becomes the basis of his deception of others.

Norman Gulley, in his work on the cosmic conflict, emphasizes that sin is fundamentally relational. Pride breaks trust. Pride distorts truth. Pride undermines love.[24] These insights align with Ezekiel's description of Lucifer's heart being "lifted up" by his own splendor. Pride does not simply alter behavior. It alters identity. It changes the internal orientation of a person toward themselves rather than toward God.

Gerhard Hasel also notes that the great controversy begins, not with an argument about power, but with a distortion of character and a redefinition of identity.[25] Lucifer's pride reshaped his understanding of himself and of God. He saw God's equality with Christ as a restriction rather than a revelation of perfect love. He saw service as limitation rather than privilege. He saw God's

---

[24] Norman R. Gulley, *Systematic Theology: Prolegomena* (Berrien Springs, MI: Andrews University Press, 2003), 248-252.

[25] Gerhard Hasel, "The Cosmic Controversy Theme in Scripture," *Journal of the Adventist Theological Society* 5.1 (1994): 27-31.

law as a boundary rather than a protection. Pride rewired the way he interpreted reality.

The seeds of pride also reveal a profound theological truth: sin begins with a lie about who God is. Lucifer could not exalt himself without diminishing God in his own mind. Pride requires a distorted picture of the Creator. Ellen White writes, "By misrepresenting the character of God, Satan has caused the world to regard Him with fear rather than love."[26] The first deception was not directed at Adam and Eve. It was directed at Lucifer himself. He believed the first lie. Only then could he speak it.

Uriah Smith observes that the rebellion began in a "contest of loyalty" in which Lucifer justified himself by questioning the justice and authority of God.[27] This early contest was not a battle of force but a battle of ideas. Pride creates an interpretive lens through which even perfect love can appear restrictive, and divine goodness can appear questionable.

From a pastoral perspective, Lucifer's fall warns every believer that pride is subtle, slow, and deeply spiritual. It operates in the inner life long before it manifests in

---

[26] Ellen G. White, *Steps to Christ* (Boise, ID: Pacific Press, 1892), 17.

[27] Uriah Smith, *Thoughts on Daniel and the Revelation* (Battle Creek, MI: Review and Herald, 1882), commentary on Revelation 12.

outward behavior. Satan did not begin his fall by accusing others. He began by redefining himself. Pride grows when we admire what God gave more than the God who gave it. It grows when our gifts become our identity. It grows when self occupies the place only God should hold.

The seeds of pride, once nurtured in Lucifer's heart, would soon blossom into the psychology of rebellion. Chapter 3 will explore how this inward corruption reshaped Lucifer's thinking, influenced his speech, and prepared the way for the accusations that would challenge the very nature of God's government.

CHAPTER THREE

The Psychology of Rebellion

S in does not appear full grown. It moves quietly, shaping thoughts long before it expresses itself in outward behavior. Lucifer's rebellion began with an inward transformation that altered the way he interpreted reality, viewed God, and understood himself. The biblical portrait of his fall shows that rebellion is fundamentally psychological before it is external. It begins in the realm of thought, desire, and interpretation. What Lucifer became outwardly was first formed inwardly.

Jesus declares that Satan "does not stand in the truth" and that "there is no truth in him" (John 8:44, ESV). The Greek expression οὐκ ἔστηκεν ἐν τῇ ἀληθείᾳ (ouk estēken en tē alētheia) literally means that he no longer abides or remains in the truth.[28] It suggests that he once stood in it but chose to depart. Rebellion began when Lucifer separated his thinking from the truth that rooted his existence in God. Once truth was displaced, illusion and self deception filled the void.

---

[28] Frederick William Danker, ed., *A Greek-English Lexicon of the New Testament and Other Early Christian Literature*, 3rd ed. (Chicago: University of Chicago Press, 2000), 391.
The verb ἵστημι ("stand, remain, be steadfast") in the perfect tense (ἔστηκεν) conveys a settled condition.
The phrase οὐκ ἔστηκεν ἐν τῇ ἀληθείᾳ indicates a refusal to remain anchored in truth.

The prophet Ezekiel explains this shift in the language of corruption: "Your wisdom and your splendor corrupted you" (Ezekiel 28:17, author's rendering). The Hebrew verb שחת (shachat) carries the meaning of ruining, spoiling, or decaying from within. Lucifer's wisdom, originally magnifying the character of God, became twisted by self focus.[29] His perception of reality changed. He no longer saw God as the source of joy and life but as a limitation to his own potential. This change in perception marks the true beginning of rebellion.

Ellen G. White captures this inner distortion with remarkable clarity. She writes, "Lucifer allowed his jealousy of Christ to prevail, and he became the more determined."[30] Jealousy is not merely an emotion. It is a way of interpreting the world. It reshapes how a person sees others and rewrites the motives they assign to them. Lucifer no longer saw Christ as the revelation of God's love. He saw Him as a rival. Pride grew into envy, and envy into suspicion.

Suspicion is the soil in which rebellion matures. Once Lucifer questioned the goodness of God, everything

---

[29] HALOT, 1458–1459; BDB, 1007. "Shachat" denotes spoil, ruin, corrupt, destroy—especially referring to moral corruption, inner decay, or twisting of what was originally good.

[30] Ellen G. White, *Patriarchs and Prophets* (Oakland, CA: Pacific Press, 1890), 36.

God did appeared to confirm his doubts. He interpreted love as control, law as restriction, and equality with Christ as injustice. The psychology of rebellion always begins with suspicion toward God's character. As J. N. Andrews observed, Lucifer "reasoned himself into unbelief."[31] Rebellion is not simply emotional. It is intellectual. It involves a reorganization of thought that seeks to justify self exaltation.

This psychological shift affected Lucifer's speech. Jesus identifies Satan as "the father of lies" (John 8:44, ESV). The Greek word ψεύστης (pseustēs) describes someone who not only speaks falsehood but creates it.[32] Lies become the natural expression of a heart that no longer abides in truth. Lucifer's own self deception became the framework for the accusations he later brought before the angels. What he whispered to himself eventually became what he whispered to others.

This reveals another essential dimension of rebellion: it spreads through influence. Thoughts shape words, and words shape communities. Ellen White notes, "He be-

---

[31] J. N. Andrews, *The Thoughts of God Toward Man* (Battle Creek, MI: Review and Herald, 1865), 42.

[32] BDAG, 1098. ψεύστης denotes a liar, deceiver, or one who falsifies reality; the term emphasizes intentional creation or propagation of falsehood.

gan to insinuate doubts concerning the laws that governed heavenly beings."[33] Lucifer did not attack openly at first. He sowed questions. He planted interpretations. He introduced alternative readings of God's character and government. Rebellion often begins, not with bold assertions, but with reframing reality through subtle misrepresentation.

The Hebrew word המד (damah), meaning to imagine or to devise, appears in contexts where thoughts become plans, and plans become action.[34] Rebellion is conceived in the imagination before it is expressed in deeds. Lucifer imagined a new order for heaven, one in which his gifts entitled him to greater authority. His imagination shaped his identity. He came to see himself as one deserving elevation. This inner narrative became the engine of his outward conflict.

Adventist scholar Ángel Manuel Rodríguez points out that Lucifer's fall shows us that sin is "self referential," meaning it turns the mind inward upon itself.[35] This

---

[33] Ellen G. White, *The Great Controversy* (Mountain View, CA: Pacific Press, 1911), 495.

[34] HALOT, 225–226; BDB, 198. "Damah" includes meanings such as to resemble, be like, imagine, devise, or consider—dependent on context and verbal stem.

[35] Ángel Manuel Rodríguez, "The Origin of Evil," *Adventist Review*, July 2007.

corresponds to the classical theological phrase incurvatus in se, the self curved inward. Lucifer's thoughts bent inward, and with that inward turning came the loss of trust, gratitude, and love. The more he focused on himself, the less he could perceive God accurately.

Norman Gulley also emphasizes the relational nature of this inward turn. Lucifer's rebellion broke his relationship with God long before he broke unity with heaven.[36] Rebellion always begins with relational disconnection. Once love is replaced by self focus, obedience becomes burdensome, and trust becomes fragile. The psychological foundation of rebellion is a heart that no longer delights in God.

Uriah Smith understood this dynamic clearly. He wrote, "Lucifer sought to elevate himself by diminishing confidence in the Creator."[37] This shows that rebellion contains both components: self exaltation and the lowering of God. The more Lucifer exalted himself, the more he misrepresented the motives of God. The more he doubted God's goodness, the more he justified his own rising ambition.

---

[36] Norman R. Gulley, *Systematic Theology: Prolegomena* (Berrien Springs, MI: Andrews University Press, 2003), 259-265.

[37] Uriah Smith, *Looking Unto Jesus* (Battle Creek, MI: Review and Herald, 1898), 112.

This inward corruption shaped Lucifer's emotions as well. Pride led to envy, which produced dissatisfaction, which resulted in resentment. Resentment grew into hostility. Hostility developed into accusation. By the time rebellion became visible, the inward transformation was complete. Lucifer no longer loved God. He no longer saw reality clearly. The psychological path of rebellion had reshaped his entire being.

The final element of the psychology of rebellion is self justification. Pride refuses correction. Ezekiel records that Lucifer's "heart was lifted up" and his wisdom corrupted, but it also implies that he resisted every divine appeal (Ezekiel 28:17). Ellen White confirms that God warned Lucifer repeatedly, yet "he persisted in his course."[38] Rebellion eventually reaches a point where correction feels like attack and truth feels like restriction. A rebellious heart interprets love as a threat.

The psychology of rebellion teaches us that sin is not merely a violation of law but a distortion of the inner life. It changes perception, identity, emotion, and relationship. It creates a self-centered framework that cannot submit to God because it no longer recognizes Him for who He is. Before Lucifer challenged God openly, he challenged God in his mind. Before he drew angels into

____

[38] Ellen G. White, *Patriarchs and Prophets*, 39.

conflict, he interpreted heaven through the lens of envy and distrust.

As we move into Chapter 4, we will see that this inward transformation prepared Lucifer to make his first public accusations against God. His psychological rebellion became verbal rebellion. What he believed internally, he would soon proclaim externally. The seeds planted in the heart became the arguments that would test the loyalty of heaven itself.

CHAPTER FOUR

The First Accusations

ebellion does not remain silent forever. What begins as inward pride and distorted perception eventually gives birth to outward expression. Jesus identifies Satan as "the accuser" in Revelation 12:10, using the Greek term κατήγορος (katēgoros), which refers to someone who brings charges in a courtroom. Accusation was not merely a habit that Satan adopted. It became the defining expression of his new identity. Once Lucifer embraced self-exaltation, his next step was to reshape the thoughts of others through accusation against God.

The first accusations were subtle. They were not shouted, nor were they introduced with open hostility. Ellen G. White describes that Lucifer "began to insinuate doubts concerning the laws which governed heavenly beings."[39] The word "insinuate" is crucial. It reveals that Lucifer's rebellion did not begin by denying God's law. It began by reframing it. He planted questions about God's motives, suggesting that the divine law was unnecessary or restrictive. Accusation often begins with questions that reshape truth rather than deny it.

The Hebrew word for slander or defamation, הלְכֻר (rekullah), conveys the idea of circulating harmful re-

---

[39] Ellen G. White, *Patriarchs and Prophets* (Oakland, CA: Pacific Press, 1890), 37.

ports.[40] In Ezekiel 28:16, God says that Lucifer was "filled with violence" by the abundance of his "trade." Many scholars understand this "trade" metaphorically as the trafficking of ideas, specifically false representations of God.[41] Lucifer carried his distorted thoughts from angel to angel. His rebellion became contagious because he spread his suspicions to others. The first accusations were not aimed at the angels. They were aimed at God.

James White notes that Lucifer "misrepresented the government of God before the angels, casting doubt upon its justice and benevolence."[42] This is the heart of the controversy. Lucifer did not attack God's power. He attacked His character. He questioned whether God's law was fair, whether Christ's position was legitimate, and whether the angels were truly free. He suggested that God's authority was rooted in self-exaltation rather than love. Ironically, Lucifer accused God of the very sin that was forming in his own heart.

---

[40] HALOT, 1278; BDB, 941. The term הָלְכֻר refers to slander, gossip, or trafficking in harmful reports—often associated with merchants who "trade" in words.

[41] See HALOT, 1278 on הָלְכֻר ("trade"), which carries a figurative sense of spreading or circulating reports, particularly slanderous ones.

[42] James White, *Review and Herald*, January 28, 1858.

Isaiah 14 reveals the internal dialogue that fueled these accusations. Lucifer said, "I will ascend above the heights of the clouds, I will make myself like the Most High" (Isaiah 14:14, ESV). His desire to ascend above others became the filter through which he interpreted God's actions. The psychology of pride shaped his theology. Because he wanted equality with Christ, he accused God of withholding it. Because he desired greater authority, he accused God of restricting him. Pride makes the heart project its own motives onto God.

Ellen White explains that Lucifer eventually argued that God's law was unnecessary for beings as exalted and intelligent as the angels.[43] Yet this idea does not rest on her writings alone. Scripture reveals the same pattern in Satan's work in Eden, where he portrayed God's command as restrictive and suggested that true wisdom and growth come through independence rather than obedience.[44] The prophets describe Lucifer exalting himself above God's order,[45] corrupt-

---

[43] Ellen G. White, The Great Controversy (Mountain View, CA: Pacific Press, 1911), 494-495.

[44] Genesis 3:4–5; see also Tremper Longman III and John H. Walton, *The Lost World of Adam and Eve* (Downers Grove, IL: InterVarsity Press, 2015), 68–70, where the authors describe the serpent undermining divine authority by presenting God's command as restrictive.

[45] Isaiah 14:13–14; John N. Oswalt, *The Book of Isaiah Chapters 1–39*

ing his wisdom through pride,[46] and rejecting the truth that anchors all created beings.[47] Early Christian thinkers such as Augustine and Aquinas recognized that Satan's fall was rooted in the desire for self rule rather than joyful submission to divine authority.[48] Even Reformation writers like Calvin and Luther understood the devil's rebellion as a rejection of God's law and government.[49] Adventist pioneers likewise observed that Lucifer promoted the idea that obedience was unnecessary for heavenly beings and that true freedom meant self direction.[50] Lucifer's subtle message was not an argument about moral behavior

---

(Grand Rapids, MI: Eerdmans, 1986), 321–323.

[46] Ezekiel 28:17; Ludwig Koehler, Walter Baumgartner, and Johann Jakob Stamm, *The Hebrew and Aramaic Lexicon of the Old Testament*, 2 vols. (Leiden: Brill, 1994–2000), 172–173, s.v. "הבג."

[47] John 8:44; G. K. Beale, *A New Testament Biblical Theology* (Grand Rapids, MI: Baker Academic, 2011), 118–121.

[48] Augustine, *The City of God*, trans. Henry Bettenson (London: Penguin, 2003), 12.6–9; Thomas Aquinas, *Summa Theologica*, I.63.2–3.

[49] John Calvin, *Institutes of the Christian Religion*, trans. Henry Beveridge (Peabody, MA: Hendrickson, 2008), 1.14.5; Martin Luther, *Lectures on Genesis: Chapters 1–5*, Luther's Works, Vol. 1, ed. Jaroslav Pelikan (St. Louis, MO: Concordia, 1958), 150–152.

[50] J. N. Andrews, "The Origin of Evil," *Review and Herald*, January 14, 1873, 52; Uriah Smith, *Thoughts on Daniel and the Revelation* (Battle Creek, MI: Review and Herald, 1882), 429–430; James White, *Review and Herald*, January 9, 1855.

but an argument about independence from God. He presented God's government as something that limited development and restrained the full expression of the creature's potential.[51]

Uriah Smith adds that Lucifer's early claims centered on the idea that "God was arbitrary in His government" and that Christ had been given undeserved superiority.[52] These charges struck at the heart of heaven's worship. If God's law was restrictive and Christ's authority unfair, then trust in God was misplaced and the nature of divine love was questionable. Lucifer was not simply sowing doubt. He was proposing an alternative vision of reality.

The Greek word πλανάω (planaō), meaning to deceive or lead astray, appears throughout the New Testament in connection with Satan. It describes not only lying but the creation of an illusion. Lucifer's accusations were crafted to make sin appear reasonable and God appear unreasonable. He used truth mixed with distortion, love mixed with suspicion, and logic mixed with pride.

---

[51] Ellen G. White, *Patriarchs and Prophets* (Oakland, CA: Pacific Press, 1890), 35–36.

[52] Uriah Smith, *Thoughts on Daniel and the Revelation* (Battle Creek, MI: Review and Herald, 1882), commentary on Revelation 12.

Deception is always most effective when it feels intellectually defensible.

Adventist scholar Jon Paulien notes that Satan's earliest attacks were "theological," not physical.[53] The controversy began with interpretations. Lucifer weaponized theology. He reimagined God's character in a way that suited his ambitions. He spoke of freedom while promoting self-exaltation. He spoke of equality while undermining divine order. He spoke of improvement while destroying the foundation of peace.

Ellen White observes that Lucifer's early work involved "exciting sympathy" among the angels.[54] He presented himself as misunderstood and mistreated. He implied that God failed to appreciate his abilities or acknowledge his contributions. Rebellion often frames itself as righteousness. Lucifer portrayed himself as the one seeking fairness and transparency, while subtly suggesting that God was withholding something essential. This tactic would later appear again in Eden when he told Eve, "God knows that when you eat of it your eyes will be opened" (Genesis

---

[53] Jon Paulien, "The Cosmic Conflict," *Adventist Review*, October 2004.

[54] Ellen G. White, *The Story of Redemption* (Hagerstown, MD: Review and Herald, 1947), 17.

3:5, ESV). The accusation was unchanged. God was holding something good back.

Gerhard Hasel explains that these early charges were attempts to redefine the meaning of God's law and reframe the meaning of divine love.[55] Lucifer argued that love did not require obedience and that freedom meant independence. This philosophical shift was the core of the first accusations. They were not about rules. They were about the nature of reality itself. If God's law was unnecessary, then God's authority was unjustified. If Christ's position was arbitrary, then God's fairness was questionable. If obedience was restrictive, then freedom meant separation from God.

The first accusations reveal a profound theological truth: sin always requires a false picture of God. No one rebels against a God they trust, love, and understand. Rebellion is sustained by misrepresentation. Lucifer's fall teaches us that error in the mind leads to corruption in the heart. Accusations against God allowed Lucifer to justify his pride, rationalize his envy, and recruit angels into his cause.

---

[55] Gerhard Hasel, "The Love of God and the Law of God," *Journal of the Adventist Theological Society* 2.1 (1991): 13-18.

This chapter prepares the way for Chapter 5, which will examine God's response to these accusations. Before war broke out in heaven, God answered the charges with transparency, mercy, and truth. Heaven witnessed not only the rise of rebellion but the revelation of God's character in response to it.

CHAPTER FIVE

The Government
of God

Every accusation Lucifer raised in heaven rested on one central question: What kind of government does God operate? At the heart of the great controversy is not a dispute over power but over character. Divine government is not based on force or arbitrary authority. Scripture reveals a kingdom established upon love, righteousness, justice, and freedom. To understand why Lucifer's rebellion challenged the very foundation of the universe, we must understand the nature of God's government before sin.

Psalm 89:14 declares, "Righteousness and justice are the foundation of Your throne; steadfast love and faithfulness go before You" (ESV). The Hebrew terms קדצ (tsedeq) for righteousness and טפשמ (mishpat) for justice describe consistency, equity, and moral reliability.[56] God's rule is predictable. It is anchored in His own unchanging character. His government expresses who He is. Because God is love, His law is love. Because God is just, His rule is just.

This stands in stark contrast to human systems, where authority often arises from dominance or self interest. The Hebrew word הָרוֹת (torah), commonly translated as "law,"

---

[56] BDB, 841–842 (tsedeq); BDB, 1047–1048 (mishpat). Both terms emphasize uprightness, moral stability, legal fairness, and covenantal faithfulness in Hebrew thought.

means instruction, guidance, or the revealed way of life.[57] God's law was not created to control but to protect and preserve the freedom of His creatures. It was the framework of joy, harmony, and communion. Ellen G. White affirms, "The law of love being the foundation of the government of God, the happiness of all created beings depended upon their perfect accord with its great principles of righteousness."[58]

Before sin, obedience was the natural expression of love. The angels did not serve under compulsion. They delighted in God's will because it was the way of life and peace. This is why Lucifer's accusations were so devastating. He suggested that God's government was rooted in self exaltation rather than self giving love. He insinuated that the angels were not truly free. These distortions required a response, not because God's authority was threatened, but because truth itself was misrepresented.

Gerhard Hasel argues that the great controversy theme shows God's government as "transparent, relational, and morally consistent."[59] God does not force obedience. He reveals Himself. He wins loyalty through truth, not

---

[57] HALOT, 1796–1797; BDB, 435. "Torah" denotes instruction, teaching, or divine guidance, not merely legal regulations—often emphasizing covenantal direction.

[58] Ellen G. White, *The Great Controversy* (Mountain View, CA: Pacific Press, 1911), 493.

[59] Gerhard Hasel, "The Cosmic Controversy Theme in Scripture," *Journal of the Adventist Theological Society* 5.1 (1994): 29.

intimidation. Lucifer's rebellion challenged this very foundation by claiming that God's law was restrictive and that equality with Christ was unfairly denied to him.

Isaiah 33:22 provides a threefold picture of divine government: "For the Lord is our judge; the Lord is our lawgiver; the Lord is our king; He will save us" (ESV). Here God is portrayed as judge (טפש, shaphat), lawgiver (קקח, chaqaq), and king (דלמ, melek).[60] These roles are united in love. God's justice is inseparable from His compassion. His authority is expressed in His desire to save, not to dominate. Lucifer's accusations attempted to split these roles apart, portraying God's authority as inconsistent with His goodness.

Ellen White describes God's character as "self denying love," and she explains that the controversy began because Lucifer misunderstood this love.[61] He interpreted divine humility as weakness and divine patience as limitation. Pride distorted his perception. Thus, the government of God became the target of his arguments. He claimed that God's law was unneeded, that Christ's role

------

[60] BDB, 1047 (shaphat = judge, to govern, to render decisions); BDB, 349 (chaqaq = to decree, inscribe, prescribe law); BDB, 572 (melek = king, ruler, sovereign authority).

[61] Ellen G. White, *Patriarchs and Prophets* (Oakland, CA: Pacific Press, 1890), 34.

was arbitrary, and that heavenly beings could live independently of divine guidance.

Norman Gulley emphasizes that divine government is unique because it is grounded in freedom.[62] God created intelligent beings with the capacity to choose, question, and even rebel. Love cannot be forced. True obedience must be voluntary. Lucifer exploited this freedom, not because God erred in giving it, but because it is inherent to love itself. The possibility of rebellion was the price of genuine freedom, but God allowed this risk because without freedom there can be no love.

James White wrote that God "ruled in justice, yet His authority was the expression of benevolence."[63] This reflects the Adventist understanding that divine justice and divine compassion are not in conflict. God's authority is not based on fear but on relationship. Lucifer framed the law as a burden and obedience as limitation. God continually revealed His character to show that His government was rooted in love.

Uriah Smith describes the rebellion as a "misapprehension of God's goodness," suggesting that Lucifer's distorted view of divine government led to an internal breakdown

---

[62] Norman R. Gulley, *Systematic Theology: Prolegomena* (Berrien Springs, MI: Andrews University Press, 2003), 301.

[63] James White, *Signs of the Times*, February 22, 1877.

of trust.[64] Trust is the glue of God's universe. When trust is broken, harmony dissolves. The purpose of divine government is to foster unity through trust. Lucifer's accusations did the opposite. They introduced suspicion, undermined confidence, and created division.

The apostle Paul writes, "Where the Spirit of the Lord is, there is freedom" (2 Corinthians 3:17, ESV). The Greek word ἐλευθερία (eleutheria) means true freedom, not autonomy from God but liberation through God. Divine government produces liberty because it aligns creatures with their Creator. Lucifer's rebellion promised independence, but independence from God leads to slavery to self, pride, and deception. What Lucifer called freedom was actually the loss of the very freedom that only God can give.

One of the central theological truths of the great controversy is that God responds to accusation with revelation. Ellen White explains that God allowed Satan to develop his arguments so the entire universe could see the contrast between truth and deception.[65] God does not silence dissent by force. He reveals His character through patience, mercy, and transparency. The angels watched as God answered accusation with love, slander

---

[64] Uriah Smith, *Looking Unto Jesus* (Battle Creek, MI: Review and Herald, 1898), 110.

[65] Ellen G. White, *Patriarchs and Prophets*, 42.

with truth, and rebellion with self revelation. This is the essence of divine government. God wins by showing.

The government of God becomes clearest at the cross, where divine love is revealed most fully. Although the cross belongs to a later chapter, it is important to note here that the principles of divine government are demonstrated throughout the entire controversy. God is patient when falsely accused. He is merciful when misunderstood. He is loving even when rejected. His law remains consistent because His character remains consistent.

Chapter 5 reveals that Lucifer's rebellion was not a conflict of power but a conflict of interpretation. He reinterpreted God's government through the lens of pride. He reframed love as limitation. He depicted obedience as servitude. By misrepresenting God's character, he attempted to undermine the moral foundation of the universe.

As we move into Chapter 6, we will examine the role of Christ, often identified in Scripture as Michael, and how His position in heaven became a central point in the controversy. Lucifer's accusations did not simply challenge the law of God. They challenged the identity, role, and authority of the Son of God. Understanding the nature of Christ and His place in God's government is essential for understanding why Lucifer's rebellion escalated into open conflict.

PART II

WAR IN HEAVEN AND THE FALL OF LUCIFER

CHAPTER SIX

The Role of Christ (Michael)

The controversy in heaven did not arise merely because Lucifer desired greater honor. It deepened when he turned his ambition against the One who already possessed that honor by divine right. Scripture reveals that the central figure in this conflict is Christ Himself, often identified in the Old Testament as Michael, the One who stands for the people of God and leads the heavenly hosts (Daniel 10:21, 12:1; Jude 9; Revelation 12:7). To understand Lucifer's rebellion, we must understand the unique role of Christ in God's government.

Christ is not a created being. He is eternal, divine, and equal with the Father. The apostle John declares, "In the beginning was the Word, and the Word was with God, and the Word was God" (John 1:1, ESV). The Greek construction θεὸς ἦν ὁ λόγος (theos ēn ho logos) explicitly identifies Christ with deity. His authority is not derived. It is inherent. His position in heaven is not granted by favoritism. It flows from His very nature as God.

Yet Scripture also portrays Christ as Michael, meaning "Who is like God." The name itself is a challenge to the claims of the enemy. The Hebrew question לְאָכִימ (mika'el) stands as a testimony to the uniqueness of God and the identity of His Son.[66] Michael appears in

---

[66] HALOT, 580; BDB, 567. The name לְאָכִימ is a theophoric question meaning "Who is like God?" emphasizing incomparability and divine uniqueness.

Scripture only in moments of conflict, judgment, and deliverance, always acting with authority that belongs only to God. He contends with Satan (Jude 9). He commands the heavenly armies (Revelation 12:7). He stands as the protector of the people of God (Daniel 12:1). These roles are divine. They belong to Christ.

Ellen G. White affirms this connection by identifying Michael as "the Son of God, the commander of the heavenly hosts."[67] The conflict between Lucifer and Christ was not a rivalry between equals. It was a rebellion against divine authority. Lucifer's dissatisfaction with Christ's position was rooted in pride and fueled by self deception. He desired a place that could never belong to a created being.

Isaiah reveals that Lucifer's ambition targeted the position held by Christ. "I will ascend above the heights of the clouds; I will make myself like the Most High" (Isaiah 14:14, ESV). The Hebrew phrase וְאֶדַּמֶּה הָמַדְּא (edammeh le'elyon) means "I will resemble" or "I will be comparable to the Most High." This was not a desire for growth or greater usefulness. It was a desire for equality with God. Christ possessed this equality by nature. Lucifer desired it by aspiration.

---

[67] Ellen G. White, *The Desire of Ages* (Oakland, CA: Pacific Press, 1898), 99.

James White explains that Lucifer "coveted the honor which belonged to the Son."[68] Uriah Smith echoes this when he writes that Lucifer "claimed a place which pertained not to him but to Christ alone."[69] These pioneer insights reflect a consistent biblical picture: the central issue of Lucifer's rebellion was Christ's identity.

The apostle Paul presents Christ as the One "in whom all the fullness of God was pleased to dwell" (Colossians 1:19, ESV).[70] The Greek word πλήρωμα (plērōma) means fullness or totality. Christ does not receive partial divinity. He possesses the whole. He is the visible revelation of the invisible God. To challenge His authority is to challenge the very nature of God's government.

Lucifer's accusations therefore targeted Christ directly. Ellen White describes that Lucifer questioned "the supremacy of the Son of God" and "sought to gain the angels to his side."[71] Lucifer framed his dissatisfaction as a call for fairness and equality. He portrayed Christ's divine position as arbitrary. He misrepresented the re-

---

[68] James White, *Review and Herald*, January 28, 1858.

[69] Uriah Smith, *Thoughts on Daniel and the Revelation* (Battle Creek, MI: Review and Herald, 1882), commentary on Revelation 12.

[70] BDAG, 828–829. πλήρωμα denotes fullness, completeness, the totality of deity and divine attributes dwelling bodily in Christ.

[71] Ellen G. White, *Patriarchs and Prophets* (Oakland, CA: Pacific Press, 1890), 36-37.

lationship between the Father and the Son. What was unity in the God, Lucifer reframed as hierarchy and favoritism.

J. N. Andrews recognized the theological depth of this conflict when he wrote that Lucifer's rebellion arose from "a blind ambition to occupy the place of Christ."[72] This ambition was rooted in pride and sustained by deception. Lucifer believed the lie he told himself. He refused to acknowledge that Christ, not he, was the rightful ruler with the Father.

Adventist scholar Ángel Manuel Rodríguez emphasizes that the conflict between Christ and Satan is "the central axis of the cosmic controversy."[73] Every other issue flows from this point. The great controversy is not primarily about angels, humans, or even the law. It is about Christ. It is about God's self revelation through His Son and Satan's determination to challenge that revelation.

In Revelation 12:7, Michael and His angels fight against the dragon. The Greek word πόλεμος (polemos) means more than physical battle. It includes conflict of ideas, words, and authority. The war in heaven was first a war

---

[72] J. N. Andrews, *The Thoughts of God Toward Man* (Battle Creek, MI: Review and Herald, 1865), 49.

[73] Ángel Manuel Rodríguez, "The Origin of Evil," *Adventist Review*, July 2007.

of arguments and only later a war of open confrontation. Christ did not fight to gain authority. He fought to uphold the truth. He fought to reveal the character of God in contrast to the distortions of Lucifer.

Norman Gulley points out that Christ's role as Michael demonstrates the self sacrificial nature of divine authority.[74] Christ does not rule through force but through revelation. His authority is expressed in service, humility, and righteousness. This is why Lucifer's accusations were so dangerous. They made divine humility appear as limitation and divine authority appear as self exaltation. He inverted the truth.

Ellen White observes that God allowed this conflict to unfold so the universe could see the character of Christ in contrast to the character of Lucifer. She writes, "The Son of God and the prince of heaven, His equal, came into conflict."[75] Her use of "equal" refers to Christ's divinity, not Lucifer's status. The contrast was essential to reveal truth. Only when Lucifer's accusations were exposed in their full nature could the universe understand the unchanging love and justice of God.

---

[74] Norman R. Gulley, *Systematic Theology: Prolegomena* (Berrien Springs, MI: Andrews University Press, 2003), 333-339.
[75] Ellen G. White, *Patriarchs and Prophets*, 36.

This chapter clarifies the central issue of the rebellion. Lucifer did not simply desire more influence. He desired the place of Christ. He wanted the worship that belonged only to God. He wanted the authority that flowed from divinity. His ambition could not be satisfied because it arose from a false understanding of himself and a distorted view of God.

As we transition to Chapter 7, we move from the tension of heavenly argument to open conflict. The war in heaven reveals what happens when pride matures into action and when deception becomes defiance. The role of Christ as Michael prepares us to understand why He alone was able to stand against the rebellion and why His victory is the foundation of all hope.

CHAPTER SEVEN

War in Heaven

The moment came when the inward rebellion of Lucifer could no longer be contained within speech, suggestion, or insinuation. What began as subtle distortions of God's character matured into open resistance. Revelation 12 describes this dramatic escalation: "Now war arose in heaven, Michael and His angels fighting against the dragon. And the dragon and his angels fought back" (Revelation 12:7, ESV).[76] The Greek term πόλεμος (polemos) means more than physical combat. It includes conflict of ideas, arguments, political challenges, and the clash of authority. The war in heaven was first theological, then relational, and only finally open conflict.

Lucifer's accusations had already divided the loyalty of angels. Ellen White describes that "a third of the angels" listened to his claims.[77] They sympathized with his grievances, misunderstood his motives, and believed God was withholding something essential. Trust was broken. Once trust collapses, unity dissolves. When it became clear that Lucifer would not turn back, and that his influence threatened the stability of heaven itself, Christ

---

[76] BDAG, 845. πόλεμος refers to war, conflict, or dispute—ranging from physical battle to ideological or verbal confrontation.

[77] Ellen G. White, *Patriarchs and Prophets* (Oakland, CA: Pacific Press, 1890), 41.

stepped forward as Michael, the defender of God's government.

Michael's leadership in this conflict shows that Christ alone possesses the authority to confront rebellion. Revelation portrays Him as leading the heavenly hosts. His authority is not delegated. It is inherent. Lucifer, now called "the dragon," resists divine authority directly. He does not submit. He fights. But this battle was not a contest between equals. It was the exposure of rebellion in contrast to righteousness.

Lucifer's fall began with pride, but the war reveals the full development of sin's nature. Jesus says Satan "was a murderer from the beginning" (John 8:44, ESV). The Greek word ἀνθρωποκτόνος (anthrōpoktonos) indicates one who destroys life.[78] Lucifer's inward corruption eventually produced a willingness to destroy others to exalt himself. The spirit of rebellion always moves toward destruction. The war in heaven exposes this trajectory.

Ellen White explains that God did not immediately destroy Satan because "the allegiance of His creatures must rest upon a conviction of His justice and

---

[78] BDAG, 88. ἀνθρωποκτόνος means murderer, one who destroys human life; used metaphorically for destructive intent or moral hostility.

benevolence."[79] If God had executed Lucifer instantly, fear would have replaced love. The universe would have obeyed from dread rather than understanding. This principle is not unique to Ellen White. Scripture itself shows that God consistently allows rebellion to reveal its nature. In Eden, the serpent was permitted to speak so that his claims could be unmasked by their consequences (Gen. 3:4–5).[80] The prophets describe Lucifer exalting himself above God's order (Isa. 14:13–14),[81] corrupting his wisdom through pride (Ezek. 28:17),[82] and rejecting the truth that anchors all created beings (John 8:44).[83] Early Christian thinkers such as Irenaeus and Augustine recognized that God allows evil to manifest itself for the sake of moral clarity.[84] Irenaeus argued that created beings learn the character of good and evil through

[79] Ellen G. White, *The Great Controversy* (Mountain View, CA: Pacific Press, 1911), 498.

[80] John H. Walton and Tremper Longman III, *The Lost World of Adam and Eve* (Downers Grove, IL: InterVarsity Press, 2015), 68–70.

[81] John N. Oswalt, *The Book of Isaiah Chapters 1–39* (Grand Rapids, MI: Eerdmans, 1986), 321–323.

[82] Ludwig Koehler, Walter Baumgartner, and Johann Jakob Stamm, *The Hebrew and Aramaic Lexicon of the Old Testament*, 2 vols. (Leiden: Brill, 1994–2000), 172–173.

[83] G. K. Beale, *A New Testament Biblical Theology* (Grand Rapids, MI: Baker Academic, 2011), 118–121.

[84] Irenaeus, *Against Heresies*, 4.37.7; Augustine, *The City of God*, trans. Henry Bettenson (London: Penguin, 2003), 12.6–9.

contrast, not coercion, and Augustine taught that God permits rebellion so that divine justice may be revealed in the open. The same principle appears in Aquinas, who wrote that evil is allowed because it exposes the superiority of God's righteousness.[85] Reformation voices affirmed this as well. Calvin described God's governance of the universe as a "public theatre" in which His justice is displayed, and Luther saw the events in Eden as God allowing Satan's arguments to play out rather than silencing him by force.[86] Adventist pioneers understood this clearly. James White wrote that "the war in heaven was the inevitable result of Satan's persistence in rebellion,"[87] and Uriah Smith observed that God permitted Satan to develop his theories so the universe could witness the nature of disobedience for themselves.[88] The conflict was not provoked by God. It was provoked by Lucifer's determination to overthrow divine authority. When persuasion failed, Lucifer escalated to open force. Pride, once planted, had matured into defiance. God

---

[85] Thomas Aquinas, *Summa Theologica*, I.49.2.

[86] John Calvin, *Institutes of the Christian Religion*, trans. Henry Beveridge (Peabody, MA: Hendrickson, 2008), 1.5.8; Martin Luther, *Lectures on Genesis: Chapters 1–5*, Luther's Works, Vol. 1 (St. Louis, MO: Concordia, 1958), 150–152.

[87] James White, *Review and Herald*, January 28, 1858.

[88] Uriah Smith, *Thoughts on Daniel and the Revelation* (Battle Creek, MI: Review and Herald, 1882), 429–431.

chose transparency over coercion so that all created beings could see, without distortion, the truth about His character and the devastating results of rebellion.

The war in heaven also reveals the relational nature of God's government. Christ did not fight alone. "Michael and His angels" fought with Him. Loyalty to Christ bound them together. Their obedience was not mechanical. It was grounded in love for His character. They fought not out of fear but out of conviction that God's way was just, righteous, and loving.

Eventually, the war reached its climax. Revelation declares that "the great dragon was thrown down" (Revelation 12:9, ESV). Heaven could no longer remain a place of peace while rebellion existed within it. The casting out of Lucifer was not an act of revenge but an act of protection. The universe needed safety. The controversy needed containment. The next chapter reveals how Lucifer was expelled and what that expulsion revealed about God and about sin.

CHAPTER EIGHT

The Fall and Casting-Out

When Lucifer and his angels were cast out of heaven, it was not merely a change in location. It was the revelation of the full consequences of rebellion. Revelation states, "He was thrown down to the earth, and his angels were thrown down with him" (Revelation 12:9, ESV). The Greek verb βαλῶ (ballō) means to cast or to remove forcefully, but in this context it signifies a decisive divine judgment. God allowed Lucifer to see what separation from Him truly means.

Ezekiel describes Lucifer's fall with painful clarity: "I cast you to the ground; I exposed you before kings" (Ezekiel 28:17, ESV). The verb דְיְתִכְלָשְׁה (hishlakhtikha) conveys the idea of sudden removal, a decisive act revealing the truth about his condition.[89] His fall was the fruit of his own choices. His exaltation of self resulted in his humiliation. Pride always collapses under its own weight.

Ellen White explains that Lucifer "saw that his disguise was torn away. His false system of government had been laid open."[90] For ages he had insisted that God's law was unfair, that divine authority was arbitrary, and

---

[89] HALOT, 1538–1539; BDB, 1017. The verb דלשׁ (shalakh/hishlik) means to cast, throw down, hurl away, or remove forcefully—often signaling decisive judgment.

[90] Ellen G. White, *Patriarchs and Prophets*, 41.

that Christ's position was unfairly granted. But when his character stood in contrast to Christ's, the universe saw that Lucifer's government was one of selfishness and deception. His exposure was necessary for the safety of all intelligent beings.

His fall also reveals the justice and mercy of God's government. God did not destroy Lucifer immediately. Ellen White explains the reason: "Had he been immediately blotted out of existence, some would have served God from fear rather than love."[91] God allowed Satan to continue living so that his character and methods would become unmistakably clear. This allowed the universe to see the contrast between the spirit of Christ and the spirit of Satan. God's justice preserves freedom. His mercy preserves choice. His patience preserves clarity.

Uriah Smith notes that Satan, even after being cast out, "still cherished hopes of ultimately succeeding."[92] This insight explains his continued activity. His rebellion was not crushed. It was redirected. Cast out of heaven, he looked for a new domain to influence. The earth, newly created and filled with promise, became the next battleground.

---

[91] Ellen G. White, *The Great Controversy*, 498.

[92] Uriah Smith, *Looking Unto Jesus* (Battle Creek, MI: Review and Herald, 1898), 115.

The fall did not change Lucifer's character. It revealed it. His hatred for Christ deepened. His envy sharpened. His accusations intensified. The war in heaven ended, but the controversy did not. It simply shifted location. Isaiah writes that Satan became the one who "made the world like a desert and overthrew its cities" (Isaiah 14:17, ESV). Deception and destruction would now mark his influence on earth.

Adventist scholar Jon Paulien points out that Satan's casting out marks a theological transition in the cosmic conflict.[93] It reveals that the controversy is no longer about convincing the angels. They have made their choice. It is now about humanity. Satan seeks to prevent humans from understanding the character of God. He brings his accusations to earth, cloaking them in temptation and deception.

The casting out of Lucifer reveals the nature of freedom in divine government. God allows beings to choose, even when they choose destruction. He restricts the spread of rebellion while preserving the right of individuals to make decisions. Love does not control. It persuades. This is why Satan was not confined immediately.

---

[93] Jon Paulien, "The Great Controversy Theme," *Adventist Review*, 2004.

The controversy must continue until all questions are answered.

Chapter 8 reveals that sin is inherently self destructive. Heaven did not destroy Lucifer. Lucifer destroyed himself. God removed him from the environment of holiness so that his rebellion would not contaminate heaven. The universe had seen enough to know that separation was necessary.

As we enter Chapter 9, we turn to the next stage of the controversy: Satan's entry into Eden, his confrontation with humanity, and the first attempt to spread his rebellion beyond the angels.

PART IV

SATAN'S FINAL STRATEGY

CHAPTER NINE

Lucifer in Eden

The garden of Eden was a place of beauty, abundance, and perfect peace. God had created an environment where humanity could flourish in fellowship with Him. Yet Eden also became the place where the controversy moved from heaven to earth. Lucifer saw in humanity an opportunity to expand his rebellion. Ellen G. White writes, "Satan determined to bring the race under his own control."[94] His strategy in heaven would now be applied to Adam and Eve.

Lucifer's approach in Eden was not a new strategy, but the continuation of the rebellion he began among the angels. Before the fall of humanity, he had already cultivated distrust in heaven by suggesting that God withheld something essential for the flourishing of His creatures. The same insinuation appears in Eden. By leading Eve to question God's goodness, Lucifer sought to reproduce in humanity the suspicion that had taken root among the angels. His goal was not only to bring Adam and Eve into disobedience. It was to bring them into his interpretation of God. Sin begins not with action but with a story, an alternative narrative about who God is and what He desires for His creatures.

The temptation in Eden was far more than an invitation to eat forbidden fruit. Scripture shows that the essence

---

[94] Ellen G. White, *Patriarchs and Prophets*, 52.

of sin is the desire to define good and evil apart from God (Genesis 3:6).[95] Eve saw that the tree was desirable for gaining wisdom, revealing that the core temptation was autonomy. The Hebrew word for wisdom often refers to moral discernment.[96] Satan was offering a counterfeit path to understanding, one that was disconnected from trust in the Creator.[97] This shows that temptation begins long before action. It begins with the invitation to reinterpret God's intentions and to view His commands as obstacles to growth rather than expressions of love.

The serpent in Genesis 3 is identified in Revelation as "that ancient serpent, who is called the devil and Satan" (Revelation 12:9, ESV). His approach in Eden mirrors his earlier methods in heaven: distortion, suspicion, and accusation. He begins with a question: "Did God actually say…?" (Genesis 3:1, ESV). The Hebrew interrogative mode challenges the reliability of God's word. This mirrors the first insinuations Lucifer made about God's law among the angels.

---

[95] John H. Walton, *The Lost World of Adam and Eve* (Downers Grove, IL: InterVarsity Press, 2015), 73–74.

[96] Ludwig Koehler, Walter Baumgartner, and Johann Jakob Stamm, *The Hebrew and Aramaic Lexicon of the Old Testament*, 2 vols. (Leiden: Brill, 1994–2000), 314, s.v. "חכם."

[97] Gerhard von Rad, *Wisdom in Israel* (Nashville, TN: Abingdon Press, 1972), 65–67.

Satan then adds an accusation: "You will not surely die" (Genesis 3:4, ESV). This directly contradicts God. The Hebrew construction לֹא־מוֹת תְּמֻתוּן (lo mot temutun) is emphatic.[98] It is not a misunderstanding. It is a deliberate denial of divine truth. Satan is not simply lying. He is reversing God's authority and inserting himself as the interpreter of reality.

His final argument reveals the heart of his deception: "God knows that when you eat of it your eyes will be opened, and you will be like God" (Genesis 3:5, ESV). This echoes Lucifer's own aspiration in Isaiah 14: "I will make myself like the Most High."[99] He projected his own motives onto God. He accused God of withholding what would elevate humanity. He framed divine love as divine limitation. This has always been the essence of his accusation.

Ellen White states, "By disguising himself as an angel of light, Satan pretended to reveal hidden truths."[100] He

---

[98] HALOT, 556; BDB, 560. The infinitive absolute with the imperfect (וּתְּמֻת תּוֹם) intensifies the negation, creating emphatic contradiction.

[99] BDB, 198. המד ("to be like, resemble, compare") is used in Isaiah 14:14 to describe Lucifer's aspiration to resemble or equal the Most High.

[100] Ellen G. White, *The Story of Redemption* (Hagerstown, MD: Review and Herald, 1947), 24.

made God appear restrictive and himself appear liberating. The psychology of rebellion he developed in heaven became the template for temptation on earth.

The serpent's method also reveals a psychological pattern that appears throughout Scripture and human history. Before Eve acted, her perception shifted.[101] She saw the tree differently. She interpreted God differently. She interpreted herself differently. This demonstrates that deception works by reshaping how the mind sees reality. Satan did not need to force disobedience. He only needed to redirect attention, reshape desire, and plant suspicion.102 This pattern lies at the heart of all temptation, where the creature begins to question God's goodness and turns inward as the source of truth.[103]

James White recognized that Eve fell because she accepted Satan's misrepresentation of God.[104] She believed that God withheld something beneficial. The original lie in heaven now became the foundational lie on earth.

---

[101] Augustine, *City of God*, trans. Henry Bettenson (London: Penguin, 2003), 13-14.

[102] Thomas Aquinas, *Summa Theologica*, I.63.2.

[103] G. K. Beale, *A New Testament Biblical Theology* (Grand Rapids, MI: Baker Academic, 2011), 119–121.

[104] James White, *Review and Herald*, February 7, 1856.

Humanity fell by believing the same doubt Lucifer first cultivated about divine goodness.

J. N. Andrews notes that the temptation in Eden was "the same principle that led to the fall of Satan," namely the belief that self exaltation leads to higher existence.[105] Satan used the tree as an instrument to reframe God's character and redirect human identity toward self determination.

The Hebrew word עָרוּם (arum), translated "crafty" or "subtle," describes the serpent's deceptive method. It does not refer to wisdom but to cunning.[106] Satan did not confront truth directly. He reinterpreted it. He presented the path of disobedience as enlightenment. He suggested that independence from God was the gateway to fulfillment.

Adventist scholar Roy Gane points out that the temptation in Eden was an attempt to redefine the nature of worship.[107] Satan offered a new authority structure

---

[105] J. N. Andrews, *The Thoughts of God Toward Man* (Battle Creek, MI: Review and Herald, 1865), 57.

[106] HALOT, 886; BDB, 791. עָרוּם denotes cleverness, shrewdness, or craftiness—context determines whether it is positive wisdom or deceptive subtlety.

[107] Roy Gane, *Leviticus, Numbers* (Grand Rapids, MI: Zondervan, 2004), 37.

where humans exalted themselves as the arbiters of right and wrong. This was the same structure he proposed in heaven, only now directed at humanity.

The events in Eden were not isolated. They were the first earthly demonstration of a cosmic conflict already underway. Revelation 12 identifies the serpent as the same adversary who deceived the angels.[108] The fall of Adam and Eve was Lucifer's attempt to extend his rebellion beyond the heavenly realm and reshape humanity into his own narrative of distrust.[109] Eden reveals that the battle is not merely about behavior. It is about interpretation, identity, and the story we believe about God.[110]

The fall in Eden reveals the tragic success of Satan's accusation strategy. Adam and Eve doubted the goodness of God. Their trust collapsed. They believed the lie that God's law was restrictive and that disobedience would bring greater freedom.

Yet the story of Eden also reveals divine mercy. God sought Adam and Eve after their fall. He provided

---

[108] Jon Paulien, *What the Bible Says About the End-Time* (Hagerstown, MD: Review and Herald, 1994), 52–54.

[109] Ángel Manuel Rodríguez, "The Origin of Evil," *Adventist Review*, July 2007.

[110] Norman R. Gulley, *Systematic Theology: Prolegomena* (Berrien Springs, MI: Andrews University Press, 2003), 255–257.

coverings. He promised a Redeemer. The controversy would now unfold on earth, but Christ would be the center of hope. As we move forward to the next chapters, the focus shifts to how Christ confronts Satan directly and how the cross becomes the ultimate answer to every accusation.

CHAPTER TEN

Lucifer and Job

The story of Job opens a rare window into the unseen conflict between Christ and Satan. Unlike Eden, where the serpent worked in disguise, the book of Job reveals the adversary entering the court of heaven to bring open accusation before God Himself. Job's experience becomes a case study in the nature of Satan's rebellion. It shows how he approaches, how he accuses, and how he interprets humanity. It also reveals that the controversy is not merely about human behavior, but about the character of God, the integrity of love, and the motives of obedience.

Job is introduced as "blameless and upright, one who feared God and turned away from evil" (Job 1:1). Scripture does not present him as perfect in sinlessness, but as perfect in integrity. Ellen White notes that Job stood as a representative of true loyalty in a world darkened by idolatry and corruption. His fidelity made him a target in the ongoing controversy. Satan approached the heavenly council not simply to discuss Job but to challenge the foundation of God's government.

The Hebrew text records that "the satan" came among the sons of God (Job 1:6). The definite article indicates a title rather than a name. The term means the adversary or the accuser. HALOT notes that the root שׂטן carries the sense of opposing, obstructing, or bringing a charge against another.[111] In the courtroom scene of Job 1, Satan stands as the prosecuting voice, accusing both God and humanity.

God declares the integrity of Job, but Satan replies with an accusation that echoes the rebellion he began in heaven. He challenges the motive behind Job's loyalty. "Does Job fear God for no reason?" (Job 1:9). This question implies that God cannot inspire genuine love. It suggests that obedience is based on self interest, not trust. Calvin observed that Satan's accusation attempts to reduce piety to a mere transaction.[112] The charge is subtle, yet devastating. If true, it would mean that God's government cannot produce sincere devotion.

Satan then asserts that God manipulates loyalty through blessing. "Have You not put a hedge around him and his house and all that he has?" (Job 1:10). The Hebrew word for hedge, שׂוּךְ (sukh), refers to a protective barrier. BDB notes that it conveys the idea of divine shelter, a shield around the righteous.[113] Satan claims that God buys love

---

[111] Ludwig Koehler, Walter Baumgartner, and Johann Jakob Stamm, *The Hebrew and Aramaic Lexicon of the Old Testament*, 2 vols. (Leiden: Brill, 1994-2000), 1305, s.v. "שׂטן."

[112] John Calvin, *Commentary on Job*, trans. Joseph Haroutunian (Grand Rapids, MI: Eerdmans, 1952), 47-48.

[113] Francis Brown, S. R. Driver, and Charles A. Briggs, *The Brown Driver Briggs Hebrew and English Lexicon* (Peabody, MA: Hendrickson, 1996), 964, s.v. "שׂוּךְ."

by surrounding His servants with prosperity. The accusation is not only against Job. It targets the righteousness of God Himself. Aquinas explained that the enemy always seeks to undermine the purity of God's goodness by attributing mixed motives to Him.[114] The controversy comes into view with clarity. Satan asserts that God's government is built on bribery, not truth.

The Lord permits Satan to test Job within limits. This moment reveals something vital about the conflict. God does not silence the accuser by force. He allows the controversy to unfold so that created beings may see the truth for themselves. Augustine taught that God permits evil to manifest its nature, so that His justice may be understood.[115] This principle is visible in Job. God does not abandon Job, but neither does He prevent the test. The controversy requires transparency and freedom. Job becomes the witness through whom God's character will be vindicated.

Satan's assault upon Job is devastating. He attacks family, possessions, and health. Yet beneath these events lies a deeper psychological conflict. Suffering often clouds perception. It raises questions of identity and worth. Job

---

[114] Thomas Aquinas, *Summa Theologica*, I.49.2.

[115] Augustine, *The City of God*, trans. Henry Bettenson (London: Penguin, 2003), 12.6.

cries out in confusion, yet he refuses to curse God. The accuser had claimed that Job's loyalty was dependent on comfort. Instead, Job remains faithful even in despair. Luther observed that Satan attacks the conscience in times of suffering, seeking to persuade believers that God has forsaken them.[116] Job's perseverance becomes a testimony to the power of genuine trust.

But the enemy does not work only through calamity. He works through interpretation. Job's friends arrive with explanations that misrepresent God. They insist that suffering must always be punishment. Their theology reflects a worldview shaped by merit, not grace. By blaming Job, they unintentionally echo Satan's argument. Ellen White notes that their counsel added to Job's trial by presenting a distorted picture of God.[117] In this way, the narrative shows that the controversy is fought not only through events, but through the ideas used to understand those events.

The turning point in Job's story comes when God speaks. The Lord does not explain the details of the controversy. Instead, He reveals His character. Job sees

----

[116] Martin Luther, *Lectures on Job*, in *Luther's Works*, Vol. 54 (St. Louis, MO: Concordia, 1967), 118-120.

[117] Ellen G. White, *Patriarchs and Prophets* (Oakland, CA: Pacific Press, 1890), 135.

the greatness of God in creation, the wisdom of His governance, and the certainty of His compassion. This revelation restores Job's identity. His questions are not dismissed, but placed within a larger reality. The God who answers him from the whirlwind is the God who sustains him in suffering. Rodríguez notes that God's response to Job shows that divine love is not proven by the absence of suffering, but by the presence of God in the midst of it.[118]

Job's vindication follows. He prays for his friends, and the Lord restores him. But the true victory occurred earlier when Job rejected Satan's accusation. Through Job, the universe witnessed that genuine faith is possible even under severe testing. Norman Gulley affirms that Job's endurance demonstrates that free beings can love God for who He is, not simply for what He gives.[119] Job stands as a witness to the truthfulness of God's character and the emptiness of Satan's charges.

The chapter prepares for the next stage in the controversy. Job resisted Satan through faith, but another would come who would confront the adversary face to face.

---

[118] Ángel Manuel Rodríguez, "Lessons from the Story of Job," *Adventist Review*, March 2010.

[119] Norman R. Gulley, *Systematic Theology: Prolegomena* (Berrien Springs, MI: Andrews University Press, 2003), 259-260.

Job points forward to Christ, the One who would meet temptation in perfect obedience. The scene in the heavenly court anticipates the greater confrontation when the Word becomes flesh and enters the battlefield Himself. As we turn to the ministry of Christ, the controversy becomes fully revealed. The accuser who stood before God to challenge Job will stand against the Son of God, and in that confrontation the destiny of the world will be decided.

CHAPTER ELEVEN

Christ Confronts Satan

The great controversy, which began in heaven, continued in Eden, and transition to Job, reached a decisive stage when Christ personally confronted Satan during His earthly life. From the moment of His incarnation, Christ entered the battleground that Lucifer had claimed. The conflict was no longer fought only through angels or prophetic revelation. It was now direct, visible, and embodied in the life of Jesus.

The incarnation was not simply the arrival of the Messiah. It was the entrance of the Commander of heaven into the enemy's territory. Scripture presents the coming of Christ as a decisive advance in the great controversy. John declares that "the Word became flesh and dwelt among us" (John 1:14), signaling that God Himself entered the field of battle.

As an infantry officer I learned that the tide of a battle shifts when the commander steps onto the field. Presence changes morale. Leadership changes momentum. Mission changes direction. In the incarnation Christ did what every great commander does. He did not direct the conflict from a distance. He entered the battlefield Himself, taking the full weight of the fight upon His own shoulders.

The incarnation unveiled the character of God within the very environment where Satan had accused Him.

The early church understood this. Athanasius wrote that Christ took humanity in order to confront the powers that enslaved it.[120] His birth in weakness was not a retreat from power. It was a strategic movement in the plan of redemption.

The book of Daniel offers a background to this moment. The heavenly "Prince" who contended with hostile spiritual forces in Daniel 10 appears again in Daniel 12 as Michael, the One who stands for the people of God. Scholars such as F. F. Bruce and Richard Bauckham note that early Christians recognized Michael as a title for the preincarnate Christ, the One who leads the armies of heaven.[121] Revelation presents the same truth. In the war against the dragon, it is "Michael and His angels" who fight (Revelation 12:7). The incarnation therefore marks the moment when the heavenly Champion steps into human history and confronts the adversary face to face.

Christ entered the world at a time of profound spiritual conflict. The Gospels indicate a heightened demonic presence, showing that Satan recognized the significance

---

[120] Athanasius, *On the Incarnation*, trans. John Behr (Yonkers, NY: St. Vladimir's Seminary Press, 2011), 54 55.

[121] F. F. Bruce, *The Epistle to the Hebrews* (Grand Rapids: Eerdmans, 1990), 14; Richard Bauckham, *Jesus and the God of Israel* (Grand Rapids: Eerdmans, 2008), 182-183.

of Christ's arrival. G. K. Beale observes that Jesus' ministry represents the beginning of the kingdom of God breaking into the world, forcing Satan into open confrontation.[122] Every miracle, every healing, every restoration of a broken life served as evidence that the power of Christ was undoing the works of the devil (1 John 3:8). The life of Jesus was therefore not a passive mission but an active invasion into enemy territory.

Ellen White affirms that Christ's entrance into the world placed Him at the center of the controversy. She writes that "Satan saw that he must either conquer or be conquered."[123] The incarnation placed the character of God and the claims of Satan in direct conflict. Love confronted selfishness. Truth confronted deception. The humility of Christ confronted the pride of the fallen cherub. From His birth onward, the enemy recognized that his accusations against the government of God were being answered not by debate, but by the life of the Son of God in human flesh.

The first major confrontation occurs in the wilderness. Matthew records, "Then Jesus was led up by the

---

[122] G. K. Beale, *A New Testament Biblical Theology* (Grand Rapids: Baker Academic, 2011), 429-430.

[123] Ellen G. White, *The Desire of Ages* (Mountain View, CA: Pacific Press, 1898), 116.

Spirit into the wilderness to be tempted by the devil" (Matthew 4:1, ESV). The Greek word πειράζω (peirazō) means to test, to scrutinize, to try someone's character.[124] Satan's goal was to provoke Christ into distrust, pride, or self-exaltation, the very path that led to his own fall. Jesus faced temptation not to prove His humanity but to reveal divine faithfulness.

Moses provides an example of this same temptation. When he struck the rock in anger rather than speaking as God commanded, he acted independently of the divine will. In that moment he placed himself in the center of the act, saying, "Shall we bring water for you out of this rock?" (Numbers 20:10). His frustration led him to assume a role that belonged only to God. Ellen White notes that Moses misrepresented the character of the Father by yielding to self and acting from impulse rather than trust.[125] This failure shows how even the most faithful leader can falter when responding from self reliance rather than dependence upon God. Christ, in contrast, resisted every invitation to act independently, revealing the perfect obedience that the controversy demanded.

---

[124] BDAG, 793–794. πειράζω means to test, tempt, examine, or make trial of—ranging from legitimate testing to malicious temptation.

[125] Ellen G. White, *Patriarchs and Prophets* (Oakland, CA: Pacific Press, 1890), 417-418.

Satan's first temptation targeted physical need: "If you are the Son of God, command these stones to become loaves of bread" (Matthew 4:3, ESV). At face value this seems harmless, but at its core it echoes Lucifer's original accusation. If God truly cared, why would His Son be hungry? Satan suggested that Christ use His divine power independently of the Father. This would break the unity of God and validate Satan's claim that God's government was restrictive.

The opening temptation reveals the nature of Satan's strategy. Matthew writes that Jesus was "tempted" by the devil (Matthew 4:1). The Greek verb πειράζω (peirazō) carries the sense of both testing and enticement. It describes an attempt to expose weakness, to probe for vulnerability, and to provoke distrust. Scholars such as R. T. France note that the temptation narrative echoes Israel's own testing in the wilderness.[126] Jesus fasts for forty days just as Israel wandered forty years. Jesus answers with Deuteronomy because He embodies what Israel failed to be. He is the faithful Son who trusts the Father in every circumstance.

---

[126] R. T. France, *The Gospel of Matthew* (Grand Rapids: Eerdmans, 2007), 129-132.

Craig Keener observes that the heart of the temptation was not bread but trust.[127] Satan sought to shift Christ's allegiance from the Father's will to His own immediate need. By attempting to provoke Jesus into acting independently, Satan repeated the very temptation that led to his own fall. He wanted Christ to grasp what He already possessed: identity, power, and legitimacy. The serpent had once told Eve that she could seize what God had already given. In the same way, Satan urges Christ to take by self assertion what the Father had already declared at His baptism: "This is my beloved Son" (Matthew 3:17).

The wilderness temptation therefore becomes a reversal of Eden. Where Adam fell in a garden of abundance, Christ stood firm in a desert of scarcity. Paul describes Jesus as the second Adam whose obedience brings life where the first Adam's disobedience brought death (Romans 5:19). Adventist pioneer E. J. Waggoner saw this moment as the foundation of Christ's victory over Satan, writing that in the wilderness "the destiny of the race trembled in the balance."[128] Christ's loyalty in weakness secured the path for humanity to overcome in Him.

---

[127] Craig S. Keener, *The Gospel of Matthew: A Socio Rhetorical Commentary* (Grand Rapids: Eerdmans, 2009), 147-148.

[128] E. J. Waggoner, *Christ and His Righteousness* (Oakland, CA: Pacific Press, 1890), 28-29.

This first temptation also reveals the nature of God's government. Satan's accusation has always been that God's law is restrictive and that obedience limits freedom. By refusing to act outside the Father's will, Christ demonstrates that true freedom is found in trusting God, not in asserting independence from Him. His response, "Man shall not live by bread alone" (Matthew 4:4), affirms that the life of the believer is sustained by the Word of God. Deuteronomy 8:3, which Jesus quotes, speaks of God teaching Israel to depend on Him rather than on their own strength. Jesus applies this truth perfectly. Where Israel doubted, He trusts. Where humanity failed, He remains faithful.

This single victory sets the trajectory for all of Christ's ministry. Satan's power thrives where the human heart distrusts God. Jesus destroys this foundation by revealing a life fully surrendered to the will of the Father. His triumph in the first temptation becomes the basis for His authority in every subsequent encounter with darkness.

Jesus responded with Scripture: "Man shall not live by bread alone" (Matthew 4:4, ESV), quoting Deuteronomy 8:3. His trust in the Father exposed Satan's lie. Christ refused to act independently. He revealed that divine love and human dependence are inseparable. Ellen G. White writes, "By trusting in God's word, Christ met every temptation."[129] The authority of Scripture defeated the accusations of Satan.

The second temptation targeted identity and presumption. Satan quoted Psalm 91, urging Christ to cast Himself down from the temple (Matthew 4:5 to 6). This was an attempt to manipulate God into action and force divine intervention. Jesus responded again with Scripture, "You shall not put the Lord your God to the test" (Matthew 4:7, ESV). Christ exposed Satan's misuse of Scripture and reaffirmed that trust does not demand proof.

The third temptation targeted worship. "All these I will give you, if you will fall down and worship me" (Matthew 4:9, ESV). This is the heart of the controversy. Lucifer desired worship in heaven and now sought it on earth. Jesus replied, "You shall worship the Lord your God and Him only shall you serve" (Matthew 4:10, ESV). The Greek word προσκυνέω (proskyneō), meaning to bow down in reverence, belongs only to God. Christ's refusal affirmed the foundation of divine government.[130]

---

[129] Ellen G. White, *The Desire of Ages* (Oakland, CA: Pacific Press, 1898), 123.

[130] BDAG, 882–883. προσκυνέω means to kneel or prostrate oneself in worship; used for both human homage and divine worship.

The final temptation strikes at the very heart of the great controversy. Matthew records that Satan offered Jesus "all the kingdoms of the world and their glory" if He would fall down and worship him (Matthew 4:8 to 9). The Greek verb προσκυνέω (proskyneō) refers to the act of prostration before a superior. It signifies surrender, allegiance, and worship. Jesus' answer, taken again from Deuteronomy, declares, "You shall worship the Lord your God and Him only shall you serve" (Matthew 4:10). In this moment the central issue of the controversy becomes unmistakably clear. Lucifer has always sought worship that belongs to God alone.

This temptation echoes Isaiah's depiction of Lucifer's ambition to ascend, to exalt his throne, and to make himself "like the Most High" (Isaiah 14:13 to 14). Scholars such as John Oswalt note that Isaiah portrays not merely political pride, but a creature attempting to seize divine authority.[131] Satan's final temptation in the wilderness is therefore not about political rule. It is the invitation for Christ to acknowledge him as the rightful ruler of the world. The very thing Satan sought in heaven he now seeks from the incarnate Son of God.

---

[131] John N. Oswalt, *The Book of Isaiah, Chapters 1 to 39* (Grand Rapids: Eerdmans, 1986), 329-331.

Beale explains that this moment reveals a cosmic legal claim.[132] Satan asserts ownership of the kingdoms of the world, although Scripture says the earth is the Lord's (Psalm 24:1). Jesus' refusal exposes the illegitimacy of Satan's authority and anticipates the restoration of divine rule. Christ will indeed inherit the nations, but only through the path of self-sacrifice rather than compromise. His kingdom comes not by seizing earthly power, but by revealing the truth about God's character.

Ellen White describes this final temptation as the climax of Satan's assault on Christ's identity.[133] Every offer was designed to cause Christ to distrust the Father and to act independently. The demand for worship reveals the motive behind Lucifer's rebellion. He seeks to replace God at the center of creation. Christ answers Satan's demand with unwavering loyalty to the Father, demonstrating that worship is not merely a religious act, but the expression of the heart's allegiance.

In refusing Satan's offer, Jesus also reveals the true nature of power in God's kingdom. Earthly dominion achieved through compromise is no victory at all. Christ

---

[132] G. K. Beale, *A New Testament Biblical Theology* (Grand Rapids: Baker Academic, 2011), 431-432.

[133] Ellen G. White, *The Desire of Ages* (Mountain View, CA: Pacific Press, 1898), 129.

conquers not by taking the throne prematurely, but by submitting to the will of the Father. This contrast between self exaltation and self sacrifice forms the moral center of the controversy. Lucifer sought a crown without a cross. Christ embraced the cross in order to reveal the character of God and restore creation. His victory in the wilderness becomes the foundation for His triumph over Satan in every future confrontation.

The dismissal of Satan after this temptation, "Then the devil left Him" (Matthew 4:11), marks not the end of the conflict but the beginning of Christ's public ministry. Luke notes that Satan departed "until an opportune time" (Luke 4:13), indicating that the adversary would return repeatedly through demonic confrontation, human opposition, and ultimately the cross. Yet the wilderness victory established that Christ would meet every assault with faith, obedience, and unwavering devotion to the Father.

James White wrote that in the wilderness Christ "wrested the scepter of earth from the usurper."[134] Satan's defeat was total. Christ succeeded where Adam failed. His victory was not for His own sake but for humanity's.

The wilderness was only the beginning. From the moment Christ entered His public ministry, Satan's hostility

---

[134] James White, *Review and Herald*, February 28, 1856.

became visible in every place where Jesus brought healing, restoration, and truth. The Gospels describe a dramatic increase in demonic activity, not because Satan gained new power, but because the presence of Christ forced the powers of darkness into the open. As Jesus preached, "Repent, for the kingdom of heaven is at hand" (Matthew 4:17), Satan recognized that his dominion over human lives was being challenged by the rightful King.

One of the clearest manifestations of this conflict is seen in the encounters with demon possessed individuals. In the synagogue at Capernaum, the demon cried out, "Have you come to destroy us? I know who You are, the Holy One of God" (Mark 1:24). Craig Keener notes that this confession reveals that the demons understood Christ's identity more clearly than many of the religious leaders.[135] They knew His coming meant the beginning of the end for Satan's rule over humanity. Jesus rebuked the spirit and delivered the man, demonstrating that His authority was not borrowed but inherent. Where Christ appeared, the kingdom of darkness retreated.

Jesus explained this reality through the parable of the "strong man." He taught that no one can plunder the

---

[135] Craig S. Keener, *The Gospel of Mark: A Socio Rhetorical Commentary* (Grand Rapids: Eerdmans, 2019), 85-87.

possessions of a strong man unless he first binds the strong man (Mark 3:27). George Ladd observes that this teaching identifies Jesus as the stronger One who has entered Satan's domain to reclaim what sin had stolen.[136] Every healing, every deliverance, every restoration was evidence that Christ was binding the adversary, limiting his influence, and undoing his works. John affirms this truth when he writes that the Son of God appeared "to destroy the works of the devil" (1 John 3:8).

Jesus also spoke directly of Satan's downfall during His ministry. When the disciples returned rejoicing that even the demons were subject to them in His name, Jesus responded, "I saw Satan fall like lightning from heaven" (Luke 10:18). This statement looks back to the original fall and forward to the ultimate defeat of the adversary. Richard Bauckham explains that Jesus speaks as the eternal Word who witnessed Lucifer's original rebellion and now announces the decisive movement toward his final ruin.[137] The ministry of Christ revealed that the kingdom of God was advancing, and Satan's hold on humanity was being broken.

---

[136] George Eldon Ladd, *A Theology of the New Testament* (Grand Rapids: Eerdmans, 1993), 70-72.

[137] Richard Bauckham, *Jesus and the God of Israel* (Grand Rapids: Eerdmans, 2008), 182-183.

Christ identified Satan as "a murderer from the beginning" and "the father of lies" (John 8:44). The Greek term ἀνθρωποκτόνος (anthrōpoktonos) emphasizes one who destroys life. Jesus exposes the murderous nature of Satan's rebellion, revealing that his hostility toward God naturally becomes hostility toward humanity. Augustine commented that Satan envies the life he cannot have and therefore seeks to corrupt the life God has given to His creation.[138] Christ's ministry manifests the opposite spirit. He restores life wherever He goes, demonstrating that the kingdom of God is rooted in self giving love rather than self exaltation.

Ellen White affirms that every act of mercy by Christ was a blow against the kingdom of darkness.[139] Jesus did not wage war through force but through compassion, truth, and obedience to the Father. Satan's kingdom thrives on fear, deception, and bondage. Christ's kingdom advances through love, clarity, and freedom. Throughout His earthly life Jesus confronted the adversary not only in moments of direct temptation, but in every instance where He lifted the burden of sin, healed

---

[138] Augustine, *Tractates on the Gospel of John*, trans. John Gibb (Edinburgh: T&T Clark, 1888), 37-38.

[139] Ellen G. White, *The Desire of Ages* (Mountain View, CA: Pacific Press, 1898), 257-258.

the sick, drove out demons, or proclaimed the truth of God's character.

These ministry confrontations prepared the way for the ultimate conflict at Calvary. Satan had failed to draw Christ into self exaltation in the wilderness and failed to prevent Him from revealing the character of God throughout His ministry. Seeing his influence slipping away, Satan moved the battle to its final ground. Christ's victory in daily life would now lead directly to His victory on the cross.

Another confrontation occurred at the cross. Jesus declared, "Now the ruler of this world will be cast out" (John 12:31, ESV).[140] The Greek term ἐκβληθήσεται (ekblēthēsetai) mirrors the earlier casting out of Satan from heaven. The cross was the second cosmic expulsion, the final exposure of Satan's character. Ellen G. White says, "In the Saviour's expiring cry, the death knell of Satan was rung."[141]

Christ confronted Satan not with force but with truth, humility, and sacrificial love. His entire ministry was a revelation of the character of God. Every healing, every

---

[140] BDAG, 311. ἐκβάλλω means to cast out, drive out, expel, or remove with authority; often used for decisive divine action.

[141] Ellen G. White, *The Great Controversy* (Mountain View, CA: Pacific Press, 1911), 503.

teaching, every act of mercy contradicted Satan's accusations. The controversy was never about power. It was about demonstrating that God is love.

As Chapter 12 will show, the cross is the central answer to every accusation ever raised against God. It is the place where the universe sees the true nature of God and the true nature of sin.

CHAPTER TWELVE

The Cross and the Great Controversy

No event in the history of the universe carries greater theological significance than the cross. It stands at the center of divine revelation, the turning point of the cosmic conflict, and the place where every accusation raised by Satan was answered with unassailable clarity. At Calvary the character of God stood fully revealed before angels, unfallen worlds, and humanity. Divine love confronted satanic rebellion. Truth confronted deception. Justice and mercy met in perfect harmony. What began in heaven and continued through the ages reached its decisive moment when Christ offered His life for the world.

Scripture gives repeated glimpses that the universe is larger than humanity alone and that other created intelligences observe the unfolding of God's purposes (Job 1:6, Luke 15:7). Early Christian thinkers such as Origen and Gregory of Nyssa taught that God created multitudes of rational beings who witness His works and learn of His character through the revelation of Christ.[142] Medieval theologians continued this understanding. Thomas Aquinas affirmed that heavenly intelligences contemplate God's actions in creation and

---

[142] Origen, *On First Principles*, trans. G. W. Butterworth (New York: Harper and Row, 1966), 2.9.

redemption with penetrating attention.[143] Reformation voices such as John Calvin recognized that angels eagerly watch the unfolding plan of salvation and study the wisdom of God revealed in Christ.[144] Modern scholarship also affirms that the cross is a public revelation, displayed not only before humanity but before the entire creation. Richard Bauckham observes that the visions of Revelation present the redemptive acts of God as cosmic disclosures before the heavenly world.[145] Even within Christian literature, John Milton portrayed unfallen intelligences as witnesses of the conflict and of the triumph achieved through Christ.[146] The cross was not hidden from the universe. It was a panoramic unveiling of divine love before every loyal intelligence in creation.

Jesus declared from the cross, "It is finished" (John 19:30). The Greek word τετέλεσται (tetelestai) expresses a completed work whose results endure.[147] It was

---

[143] Thomas Aquinas, *Summa Theologica*, trans. Fathers of the English Dominican Province (New York: Benziger Brothers, 1947), I.61.

[144] John Calvin, *Commentaries on the Catholic Epistles*, trans. John Owen (Grand Rapids, MI: Eerdmans, 1948), 293.

[145] Richard Bauckham, *The Theology of the Book of Revelation* (Cambridge: Cambridge University Press, 1993), 34-36.

[146] John Milton, *Paradise Lost*, in *The Complete Poetry and Essential Prose of John Milton*, ed. William Kerrigan, John Rumrich, and Stephen M. Fallon (New York: Modern Library, 2007), Book 3.

[147] BDAG, 996. τετέλεσται (perfect tense of τελέω) means "it has been completed," "brought to its intended goal," or "fulfilled fully."

not the lament of a dying teacher but the triumphant proclamation of the Son of God. Christ completed the mission entrusted to Him by the Father. He fulfilled the covenant promises. He unmasked the character of Satan. He revealed the foundation of God's government as self giving love. Nothing Satan had claimed could stand before the revelation given at Calvary.

Ellen G. White affirms that "the cross was Heaven's answer to Satan's charges."[148] Every argument Lucifer presented in heaven, every distortion whispered to the angels, and every accusation hurled at God's people across the ages was confronted and answered by the self sacrificing love revealed at the cross. The entire controversy reaches its moral climax here, for the cross displays what Satan refused to believe: that God is love.

Paul describes this triumph in striking cosmic terms. "He disarmed the rulers and authorities and put them to open shame, triumphing over them in Him" (Colossians 2:15). The verb translated "to expose publicly" comes from δειγματίζω (deigmatizō).[149] Paul compares the cross to a public victory procession in which the defeated enemies of a king were displayed openly. Here the spiritual pow-

---

[148] Ellen G. White, *The Desire of Ages*, 761.

[149] BDAG, 214. δειγματίζω means to expose, disgrace, or make a public example of.

ers aligned with Satan stood revealed as powerless in the presence of Christ's sacrificial victory. What Satan tried to conceal for ages was made visible before the universe.

This defeat touches not only the spiritual powers but the moral and legal claims Satan made against God's government. He accused God of being arbitrary, yet at the cross God Himself bore the consequences of sin. He claimed that God was unwilling to sacrifice, yet at the cross Christ gave everything. He claimed the law was restrictive, yet at the cross Jesus obeyed to the point of death and showed that obedience flows from love.

Adventist pioneers saw these connections clearly. James White called the cross "the most wonderful exhibition of God's love man or angel has ever witnessed."[150] Uriah Smith described Calvary as "the eternal refutation of Satan's charges."[151] Their emphasis was not on abstract theology but on the revelation of God's character. The cross does not merely redeem humanity. It vindicates God.

Modern scholarship supports this understanding. Gerhard Hasel explains that the cross demonstrates both

---

[150] James White, *The Law and the Gospel* (Battle Creek, MI: Review and Herald, 1870), 42.

[151] Uriah Smith, *Looking Unto Jesus* (Battle Creek, MI: Review and Herald, 1898), 198.

divine justice and divine mercy "without compromising either."[152] God upheld the moral order of the universe while opening the pathway of salvation for fallen humanity. Satan insisted that such harmony was impossible. At the cross justice and mercy met, revealing the depth of God's law and the depth of God's love.

The cross also exposes the destructive nature of sin. Sin kills. Sin deceives. Sin separates. When Christ bore the sin of the world, Satan's system of rebellion stood revealed. Scripture describes him as "a roaring lion, seeking whom he may devour" (1 Peter 5:8), and Calvary showed that this description is not metaphor alone but the reality of his character. The universe saw that Satan would destroy the innocent to preserve his claims. He devours through deception and consumes through pride, fear, and accusation. Ellen White writes that "Satan saw that his disguise was torn away. His character stood revealed." [153] All sympathy for him ended. Heaven recognized that the rebellion was rooted not in misunderstanding but in deliberate hatred of God's character and government.

The resurrection confirms everything accomplished at the cross. Paul declares that Christ "was raised for

---

[152] Gerhard Hasel, "The Cross and the Cosmic Conflict," *Journal of the Adventist Theological Society* 4, no. 2 (1993): 34-39.

[153] Ellen G. White, *The Great Controversy*, 502.

our justification" (Romans 4:25). The empty tomb is Heaven's affirmation that the sacrifice was accepted and that Satan's defeat is irrevocable. Jesus rises not as a victim of satanic hatred but as the triumphant Redeemer who holds the keys of death and the grave (Revelation 1:18). Death, Satan's greatest weapon, cannot hold Him.

Together the cross and the resurrection form the decisive turning point in the great controversy. Every accusation Lucifer raised has been fully answered. The law is shown to be perfect and just. God is revealed as self sacrificing love. The universe sees that the throne of God is established not by power but by goodness.

In this moment Christ became both the offering for sin and the One who presents that offering before the Father. His blood stands as the eternal testimony of God's love and the guarantee of our redemption. Scripture says that "we have redemption through His blood" (Ephesians 1:7), and the book of Hebrews describes Christ entering the heavenly sanctuary "by means of His own blood" (Hebrews 9:12). He claims His sacrifice on our behalf, and we, by faith, claim the merits of that sacrifice as our hope and assurance. His blood becomes our plea, our covering, and our confidence in the presence of God.

The controversy is not yet finished, but its outcome is certain. Christ has defeated the adversary. What remains is the eradication of sin forever and the restoration of the universe to harmony under the eternal reign of divine love. Chapter 13 will describe how the final judgment completes the work begun at Calvary and brings the great controversy to its rightful end.

CHAPTER THIRTEEN

The Final
Eradication of Evil

The great controversy does not end at the cross. It ends when sin is eradicated and the universe is restored. Scripture gives a clear picture of the final judgment and the destruction of evil. The controversy began with rebellion in heaven, moved to earth, climaxed at the cross, and will conclude with the removal of sin from the universe forever.

John describes the final end of Satan with solemn clarity. "And the devil who had deceived them was thrown into the lake of fire" (Revelation 20:10, ESV). Fire in Scripture often symbolizes purification and final judgment. It is the cleansing of creation from the last trace of rebellion. This is not arbitrary vengeance. It is the natural conclusion of sin. Sin is incompatible with life. Separation from God is destruction.

The Hebrew word הָלַךְ (kalah), meaning to complete or bring to an end, appears in Isaiah's description of the final judgment. "A full end is decreed" (Isaiah 10:23, ESV). God brings sin to its conclusion not simply to punish, but to preserve the universe from further harm. Evil had a beginning. It must also have an end.[154]

------

[154] Ludwig Koehler, Walter Baumgartner, and Johann Stamm, *The Hebrew and Aramaic Lexicon of the Old Testament*, volumes 1 and 2 (Leiden: Brill, 1994 to 2000), 480-481.

Francis Brown, S. R. Driver, and Charles A. Briggs, *The Brown Driver Briggs Hebrew and English Lexicon* (Peabody, MA: Hendrickson, 1996), 477.

Ellen G. White explains, "The destruction of sin and sinners is the final act of God's mercy."[155] This is a profound theological truth. God does not destroy because He is angry. He destroys because love cannot allow suffering to continue forever. To permit sin to endure eternally would perpetuate pain for all creation. The eradication of sin is the restoration of peace.

This final act of judgment is also an act of mercy, even toward those who are lost. Revelation describes the wicked crying out for the mountains and rocks to fall on them (Revelation 6:16, ESV). This is not God tormenting them. It is the expression of their own desire to escape the presence of the Lamb. The glory that brings life to the redeemed brings anguish to those who have chosen separation. In the end they recognize the truth, yet they cannot endure the holiness they once rejected. God grants them the very thing they plead for, allowing them to cease rather than continue in terror of the One whose presence they have refused. Their destruction is not God crushing them against their will, but God honoring their final choice with solemn mercy.[156]

----

[155] Ellen G. White, *The Great Controversy* (Mountain View, CA: Pacific Press, 1911), 543.

[156] Ellen G. White, *The Great Controversy* (Mountain View, CA: Pacific Press, 1911), 541–543.
See also Richard Bauckham, "The Justice of God in the Book of Revelation," in *The Climax of Prophecy* (Edinburgh: T and T Clark,

Christian theologians throughout history recognized this same pattern. Augustine taught that the universe cannot be healed until evil is finally removed.[157] Aquinas argued that separation from God is the natural end of a will fixed against Him.[158] Calvin wrote that Christ reigns until all enemies, including death itself, are destroyed.[159] Luther affirmed that the devil is mortally wounded at the cross but fights until the final judgment.160 Their witness confirms that the cross secured decisive victory, but the end of evil comes only at the restoration of all things.

1993), 276–285, who argues that the wicked flee from God's presence because holiness is unbearable to a will fixed against Him.

[157] Augustine, *The City of God*, translated by Henry Bettenson (London: Penguin, 2003), book 20, sections 1-3.

[158] Thomas Aquinas, *Summa Theologica*, part 1, question 64, articles 1-2.

[159] John Calvin, *Commentary on the First Epistle to the Corinthians*, translated by John Pringle (Grand Rapids, MI: Baker, 2003), pages 490-495 on First Corinthians 15 verses 24-26.

[160] Augustine, *The City of God*, translated by Henry Bettenson (London: Penguin, 2003), book 20, sections 1-3.

Thomas Aquinas, *Summa Theologica*, part 1, question 64, articles 1-2.

John Calvin, *Commentary on the First Epistle to the Corinthians*, translated by John Pringle (Grand Rapids, MI: Baker, 2003), pages 490-495.

Martin Luther, *Lectures on Genesis. Chapters 6 to 14*, in *Luther's Works*, volume 2 (Saint Louis, MO: Concordia, 1960), 188-190.

Adventist scholar Norman Gulley emphasizes that the final judgment is relational.[161] God does not execute arbitrary punishment. He honors human choice. Those who reject His presence ultimately experience the natural result of separation from the source of life. Lucifer, who first stepped away from God, experiences the full consequence of that decision in the end.

James White wrote that the final destruction of evil "secures the universe in eternal safety."[162] With sin gone, there is no more threat, no more deception, no more accusation. The universe is united again under God's government of love.

Malachi describes the righteous standing on "ashes under the soles of your feet" (Malachi 4:3, ESV). This is not triumphalism. It is symbolic language demonstrating the finality of evil. Evil leaves no seed of future rebellion. It has no voice, no claim, and no continuing life. It is completely gone.

After the eradication of sin, God creates "new heavens and a new earth" (Isaiah 65:17, ESV). The Greek word kainos in Revelation 21:1 emphasizes renewal rather

---

[161] Norman R. Gulley, *Systematic Theology. Eschatology* (Berrien Springs, MI: Andrews University Press, 2013), 247.

[162] James White, "The Destruction of the Wicked," *Signs of the Times*, June 25, 1874.

than simple replacement. Creation becomes fresh, untainted, restored to its original purpose. Unfallen angels and other created worlds, who watched the controversy unfold, behold the universe in harmony once again.[163]

Ellen White describes the closing scene with breathtaking beauty. "The great controversy is ended. Sin and sinners are no more. One pulse of harmony and gladness beats through the vast creation."[164] God's character stands vindicated. His law is shown to be just. His government is revealed as love.

With evil eradicated, God dwells again with His people. "He will wipe away every tear from their eyes" (Revelation 21:4, ESV). The controversy closes not with fear or force but with comfort and restoration. Love triumphs. Life begins anew throughout the universe.

---

[163] Gerhard F. Hasel, "The End of the Controversy," *Journal of the Adventist Theological Society* volume 5 number 2 (1994): 90-92.
[164] White, *The Great Controversy*, 678.

CHAPTER FOURTEEN

God Vindicated Forever

The great controversy began with a question. It will end with a revelation. Throughout the ages Satan has misrepresented God's character, claiming that His law is restrictive, His authority arbitrary, and His government rooted in control rather than love. But Scripture declares that God will bring the conflict to a close not through force, but through full and undeniable vindication of His character before the entire universe.

The prophet Nahum writes, "Affliction shall not rise up the second time" (Nahum 1:9, ESV). The Hebrew word סוק (qum), meaning to arise or stand, is used here in a negative sense.[165] Evil will never again stand or reestablish itself. God's response to rebellion is not merely to remove sin but to resolve it in such a way that the universe will never again question His justice or His love.

This vindication is grounded in the revelation of God's character through Christ. Jesus told Philip, "Whoever has seen Me has seen the Father" (John 14:9, ESV). In Christ every accusation against God is answered. The Greek verb ὁράω (horaō), meaning to see or perceive, emphasizes more than physical sight. It means to grasp,

---

[165] HALOT, 1082–1084; BDB, 877–879. סוק means to rise, stand, arise, establish; used here negatively to signify that evil will never stand or reappear again.

comprehend, or understand.[166] To see Christ is to understand the Father's heart. The universe has witnessed this revelation at the cross, through the gospel, and finally through the destruction of sin.

Ellen G. White describes the conclusion of the controversy with profound clarity:

"When the controversy is ended, the character of God is seen in all its glory. Love has conquered."[167] This is the core of Adventist theology. The controversy ends with the justification of God's character before all creation.

The apostle Paul presents the final vindication in universal language: "At the name of Jesus every knee should bow... and every tongue confess that Jesus Christ is Lord" (Philippians 2:10-11, ESV). The Greek verb ἐξομολογέω (exomologeō) means to confess openly, to acknowledge truth with clarity and conviction.[168] This is not forced worship. It is universal recognition that God has been right from the beginning.

---

[166] BDAG, 719–720. ὁράω means to see, perceive, recognize, or understand—often with the sense of spiritual comprehension.

[167] Ellen G. White, *The Great Controversy* (Mountain View, CA: Pacific Press, 1911), 678.

[168] BDAG, 348. ἐξομολογέω means to confess, acknowledge openly, praise, or declare one's agreement.

Uriah Smith understood this principle well. He wrote, "The whole universe will finally acknowledge the justice of God, not by compulsion, but because evidence leaves no ground for doubt."[169] The controversy ends not with fear but with understanding. God does not seek submission through power. He seeks acknowledgment through revelation.

J. N. Andrews emphasized the same truth, noting that "the judgment reveals the righteousness of God as clearly as it reveals the guilt of the wicked."[170] In the final judgment God does not merely condemn evil. He reveals the transparency of His dealings. Every question is answered. Every doubt resolved. Every being sees the fairness of His decisions.

Adventist scholar Ángel Manuel Rodríguez describes the final resolution as "God opening His character to the universe for examination."[171] In this openness lies the beauty of divine governance. God does not fear scrutiny. He invites it. The controversy is not settled by decree but by demonstration.

---

[169] Uriah Smith, *Looking Unto Jesus* (Battle Creek, MI: Review and Herald, 1898), 215.

[170] J. N. Andrews, *The Judgment: Its Events and Their Order* (Battle Creek, MI: Review and Herald, 1890), 87.

[171] Ángel Manuel Rodríguez, "The Vindication of God," Biblical Research Institute Paper, 2005.

Revelation presents a scene of cosmic harmony: "And I heard every creature... saying, 'To Him who sits on the throne and to the Lamb be blessing and honor and glory and might forever'" (Revelation 5:13, ESV). The Greek word εὐλογία (eulogia), meaning blessing or praise, signifies joyful acknowledgment of God's goodness. Creation joins in unanimous worship because the truth about God has been fully revealed.

After the eradication of sin, God creates "new heavens and a new earth" (Revelation 21:1, ESV). The Hebrew prophets and the apostolic witness join in this hope. Isaiah says, "The former things shall not be remembered or come into mind" (Isaiah 65:17, ESV). This does not mean memory is erased. It means pain no longer wounds, and fear no longer threatens. The universe stands in the security of God's unchanging love.

Ellen White paints the final scene beautifully:

"One pulse of harmony and gladness beats through the vast creation."[172]

The universe is unified because the truth has been revealed. God's character, questioned by Lucifer, misunderstood by humanity, and distorted throughout history, shines with unclouded brilliance. His law stands

---

[172] Ellen G. White, *The Great Controversy*, 678.

vindicated. His love stands triumphant. His justice stands unshaken.

James White expressed this very hope:

"When the great controversy closes, the moral harmony of the universe will shine more brightly for having passed through the shadow."[173] He saw the controversy not as a disruption of God's purposes but as the stage through which His character becomes eternally secure in the affections of His creatures.

J. N. Andrews likewise wrote, "The universe will forever adore God for the justice and mercy revealed in His dealings with sin."[174] Redemption and judgment both testify to His character.

The great controversy closes not with fear or sorrow, but with worship. Revelation describes God dwelling with His people: "He will wipe away every tear from their eyes" (Revelation 21:4, ESV). This is the final answer to suffering. God does not merely end pain. He restores joy. He does not erase the story of sin. He redeems it and places it within the larger narrative of His faithfulness.

---

[173] James White, *Review and Herald*, April 9, 1861.

[174] J. N. Andrews, *The Thoughts of God Toward Man* (Battle Creek, MI: Review and Herald, 1865), 72.

The final vindication of God's character is the foundation for eternal peace. The universe will never again question His justice because it has seen the truth for itself. Love forms the eternal bond between God and His creation. The controversy ends, not with domination, but with relationship restored.

As you enter the final sections of this work, Chapter 14 stands as the crown of the book's message.

God wins because love proves supreme.

God is vindicated because His character is seen in its full light.

The universe is secured because every doubt has been answered and every question resolved.

PART IV

SATAN'S FINAL STRATEGY

Part IV turns from the cosmic storyline to its modern battlefield. The themes that shaped Lucifer's fall, the identity crisis in Eden, and the conflict revealed at the cross continue in the digital age with renewed intensity. What Chapter 14 revealed as the theological crown of the controversy, Part IV now applies to contemporary life. The same inward curve that corrupted Lucifer and the same distortions of God's character that fueled the rebellion now appear in new forms shaped by technology, self-expression, distraction, and digital identity. These final chapters show that the great controversy is not only a past or future drama but a present reality unfolding in the minds and habits of humanity today.

CHAPTER FIFTEEN

The Digital War for the Human Mind

If the cross revealed Satan's defeat, the modern world reveals his desperation. Revelation describes Satan as having great wrath because he knows his time is short (Revelation 12:12, ESV). As the controversy nears its final movements, the enemy's strategy shifts from open attack to subtle infiltration. The digital age becomes the arena where the battle for the mind intensifies.

The conflict that began in heaven continues with renewed intensity in the modern world. Although the technology of today would have been unimaginable to earlier generations, the spiritual forces behind it have not changed. Scripture presents the great controversy as a battle for attention, loyalty, identity, and worship. The dragon seeks devotion, not primarily through fear, but through the quiet redirection of the human mind. The same methods that corrupted Lucifer in heaven now saturate digital culture with subtle and pervasive influence.

The Continuity of Satan's Methods

Revelation describes the devil as the one who deceives the whole world (Revelation 12:9). His strategies remain constant. Pride, accusation, self focus, and identity distortion are the defining features of his rebellion. These movements that shaped Lucifer's fall now appear in the spiritual atmosphere of the last days. Paul warns Timothy that society will become lovers of self, lovers of pleasure, proud, arrogant, without self control, and possessing the appearance of godliness while denying its power (2 Timothy 3:2-5). This portrait reflects the inward curve that corrupted Lucifer in heaven. What began in his heart now becomes the dominant spirit of the age.

Ellen G. White recognized this pattern with clarity. She wrote that Satan invents every possible device to engross the mind.[175] Her words describe the very crisis of the digital world. Distraction is not neutral. It shapes devotion, attention, and worship.

Identity and the Revival of the First Lie

The first temptation in Eden was not simply about fruit. It was an invitation to redefine identity apart from God. "You will be like God" (Genesis 3:5). The serpent redirected Eve's attention from the Creator to herself. This deception echoes the transformation that took place in Lucifer's own heart. He desired divine prerogatives

---

[175] Ellen G. White, *The Great Controversy* (Mountain View, CA: Pacific Press, 1911), 519.

without divine character. Augustine later identified this inward turn as the soul's curve toward itself.[176]

Christian theologians throughout history have described the essence of sin as incurvatus in se, the soul curved inward on itself. Augustine used this expression to explain how pride collapses the heart away from God and toward self-absorption.[177] Luther expanded this idea, teaching that the human will bends inward until the self becomes its own center.[178] Calvin wrote that the sinful heart becomes a workshop of idols because it seeks its own glory rather than the glory of God.[179] This inward curve began with Lucifer. Once he turned his attention from the character of God to the elevation of self, his entire being bent toward pride, suspicion, and self exaltation. The same inward turn appears in Eden and continues in every age. Christ reveals the opposite direction of life, the outward movement of self giving love. The

---

[176] Augustine, *Confessions*, trans. Henry Chadwick (Oxford: Oxford University Press, 1991), 98-99.

[177] Augustine, *On the Trinity*, trans. Edmund Hill (Brooklyn, NY: New City Press, 1991), 12.11.

[178] Martin Luther, *Lectures on Romans*, in *Luther's Works*, vol. 25, ed. Hilton C. Oswald (St. Louis: Concordia, 1972), 291.

[179] John Calvin, *Institutes of the Christian Religion*, trans. Henry Beveridge (Peabody, MA: Hendrickson, 2008), 1.11.8.

entire great controversy is the collision between these two directions of the soul.

The digital environment magnifies this temptation. It encourages individuals to construct identities based on image, performance, and social approval. The self becomes something crafted rather than received. Theologian Alister McGrath notes that modern culture has replaced transcendence with expressive individualism, making the self the final authority.[180] This cultural shift mirrors Lucifer's ambition to define himself independently of the Creator.

Attention as the Center of Worship

The Bible consistently connects worship with attention. The psalmist meditates on the law of the Lord day and night (Psalm 1:2). Jesus teaches that the heart follows whatever captures one's treasure (Matthew 6:21). Paul calls believers to set their minds on things above (Colossians 3:2). Worship is not limited to outward practices. It is the orientation of the mind and the devotion of the heart.

The digital world challenges this biblical picture by demanding constant attention. Notifications, entertainment,

---

[180] Alister McGrath, *The Twilight of Atheism* (New York: Doubleday, 2004), 135.

information, and messages compete for the mind's focus. Cultural critic Neil Postman argued that modern technology reshapes how people think, learn, and believe.[181] In this environment, the enemy does not need to silence the voice of God. He only needs to drown it out.

Ellen White affirms that the mind is the battlefield on which the greatest conflict between good and evil is taking place.[182] Satan uses distraction as a primary weapon because it weakens discernment, confuses identity, and breaks the rhythm of communion with God.

The Appearance of Godliness Without Power

Paul describes a generation that possesses the appearance of godliness while lacking its power (2 Timothy 3:5). Digital culture makes this deception easy. One can share verses, post devotionals, follow religious accounts, and display faith online while lacking a living connection with Christ. Digital platforms encourage spiritual performance without transformation.

---

[181] Neil Postman, *Amusing Ourselves to Death* (New York: Penguin, 1985), 16-29.

[182] Ellen G. White, *Mind, Character, and Personality*, vol. 1 (Nashville, TN: Southern Publishing, 1977), 73.

Ellen White warns that many hold the form of godliness while lacking the power of a renewed life.[183] Adventist pioneers also recognized this danger. James White wrote that true religion rests upon surrender and obedience, not merely upon profession.[184] The digital age magnifies the temptation to adopt the form of faith without its spiritual depth.

Comparison Culture and the Echo of Lucifer's Fall

Comparison is one of the most destructive features of digital life. It creates insecurity, envy, pride, and self obsession. Scripture describes Lucifer's heart as lifted up because of his beauty and his wisdom as corrupted by self admiration (Ezekiel 28:17). The more he looked inward, the less he could see God. The digital mirror performs the same work in human hearts.

Psychologists warn that social media platforms encourage a constant measurement of worth through likes, comments, and visibility. Users are drawn into feedback loops where identity becomes defined not by character or relationship with God but by what others approve. One

---

[183] Ellen G. White, *The Desire of Ages* (Mountain View, CA: Pacific Press, 1898), 309.

[184] James White, *Gospel Works* (Battle Creek, MI: Review and Herald, 1870), 112.

study found that young people who frequently sought social-media feedback displayed higher levels of depressive symptoms.[185] Another investigation concluded that upward comparisons, viewing others as superior in "followers" or "engagement," mediate the link between problematic social media use and poor self-esteem.[186] The U.S. Surgeon General's Advisory reports that for adolescents especially, digital metrics become a substitute for authentic belonging and internal worth.[187] This culture mirrors the inner spiritual dynamic of the inward curve toward self-exaltation. What corrupted the angelic being now subtly corrupts the inner lives of millions.

Algorithms as Unseen Instructors

Digital platforms do not simply deliver content. They shape desire. Algorithms act as unseen instructors that

---

[185] Jessica Nesi, "Using Social Media for Social Comparison and Feedback Seeking: Gender and Popularity Moderate Associations with Depressive Symptoms," *Journal of Abnormal Child Psychology* 43 (2015): 405–417, https://doi.org/10.1007/s10802-014-9953-9

[186] Aisha Samra et al., "Social Comparisons: A Potential Mechanism Linking Problematic Social Media Use with Depression," *Frontiers in Psychology* 13 (2022): 1–12, https://doi.org/10.3389/fpsyg.2022.917393

[187] U.S. Department of Health & Human Services, "Social Media and Youth Mental Health: The U.S. Surgeon General's Advisory," (Washington, DC: HHS, 2023).

train the mind by repetition, exposure, and emotional reinforcement. Although these systems are not moral beings, they magnify the tendencies of human nature and reward impulses that weaken spiritual resilience.

Jacques Ellul notes that modern technology reshapes habits and thought far more deeply than people realize.[188] The digital world creates a context in which spiritual attention becomes fragmented, prayer becomes difficult, and the voice of God is overshadowed by noise.

The Three Angels in a Digital World

Revelation 14 contains the clearest divine response to a world shaped by self worship and distraction. The first angel calls humanity to fear God, give Him glory, and worship the Creator (Revelation 14:7). This call confronts the spirit of expressive individualism. The second angel exposes the confusion of Babylon, a system built on pride and deception. The third angel warns of the disastrous results of giving allegiance to human authority rather than divine truth.

Ellen White explains that Satan continually seeks to misrepresent God and direct the mind away from Christ.[189]

---

[188] Jacques Ellul, *The Technological Society* (New York: Vintage Books, 1964), 125-140.

[189] Ellen G. White, *Steps to Christ* (Mountain View, CA: Pacific Press, 1892), 72.

The Three Angels Message offers the antidote. It restores God as the center of identity, the focus of worship, and the foundation of truth.

The Call of Christ in a Distracted World

The gospel calls the believer into a life that resists the spirit of the age. Jesus invites His followers to deny self, take up the cross, and follow Him (Matthew 16:24). True discipleship demands intentional surrender. Uriah Smith wrote that obedience begins where self ends.[190] The digital world elevates self. Christ calls the believer to crucify it.

To follow Christ today is to choose communion over noise, prayer over distraction, Scripture over scrolling, and worship over self-display. The people who stand with the Lamb at the end of time follow Him wherever He goes (Revelation 14:4). Their lives are shaped by His character rather than by the pressures of digital culture.

The Final Victory of God's Love

The great controversy concludes with worship restored to its rightful center. Satan's goal has always been to turn the heart inward. Christ's victory is to turn the

---

[190] Uriah Smith, *Thoughts on Daniel and the Revelation* (Battle Creek, MI: Review and Herald, 1882), 433.

heart upward toward God and outward in love for others. Although the digital age is filled with unprecedented challenges, the call of Christ remains unchanged. Fix your attention on the Lamb. Behold His character. Follow Him wherever He leads.

The final generation will stand not because they avoided technology, but because they learned to guard the mind, surrender the heart, and live with undivided devotion to Christ. Their lives testify that even in a world shaped by self-worship, the power of God can transform the heart. The controversy ends with the universe restored and with worship once again directed to the Creator, the Redeemer, and the Lamb who triumphs through love.

The digital age does not replace the great controversy. It accelerates it. The same forces that led Lucifer to exalt himself now shape the identities, desires, and distractions of modern life. But Scripture teaches that the controversy does not end with cultural trends or psychological influence. It ends with the judgment of God, where every motive is revealed and every question is answered. What follows in Chapter 16 lifts the reader from the digital battlefield back to the cosmic courtroom, where the final movements of the controversy unfold.

CHAPTER SIXTEEN

The Judgment and the Eradication of Sin

As the controversy approaches its final scenes, Scripture shifts the focus from Satan's deception to God's justice. If the digital age reveals the intensity of Satan's last efforts, the judgment reveals the clarity of God's final answer. Revelation portrays a moment when every hidden thing is brought to light, every question is settled, and the universe sees the full transparency of God's government. The same God who won our hearts at Calvary now reveals the fairness of His decisions before all creation.

The judgment is not an abstract doctrine or a threat to the believer. It is the divine process through which God restores justice, exposes truth, defends His people, and brings the great controversy to its rightful end. Scripture portrays God's judgment as both transparent and redemptive. "For the Lord is a God of justice" (Isaiah 30:18, ESV). His judgments reveal His character and secure the universe in eternal safety.

Daniel presents the investigative phase of judgment with solemn beauty:

"I watched till thrones were placed, and the Ancient of Days took His seat" (Daniel 7:9, ESV). The Hebrew word דִּין (din), meaning to judge or govern, emphasizes a courtroom where truth is examined, not imposed. God does not judge in secrecy.[191] Daniel says that "the court sat in judgment, and the books were opened" (Daniel 7:10, ESV). This imagery reveals divine transparency. Heaven examines the evidence not because God needs information but because the universe does.

Ellen G. White describes the investigative judgment as a process where "the character of every person is examined before all."[192] This judgment reveals who has chosen loyalty to Christ and who has embraced the principles of Satan. It does not determine who God wants to save. It reveals who has chosen to be saved.

Christian theologians throughout history recognized that divine judgment is not God deciding whom He prefers but God revealing what each person has freely chosen. Augustine taught that the judgment discloses the true orientation of the heart, showing whether the soul has turned inward toward self or outward toward God.[193] Thomas Aquinas argued that God's judgment is "manifestation," not manipulation, for the judgment reveals the inner reality of a person's will rather than imposing

---

[191] Ludwig Koehler, Walter Baumgartner, and Johann Stamm, *The Hebrew and Aramaic Lexicon of the Old Testament*, vol. 1 (Leiden: Brill, 1994), s.v. "דִּין."

[192] Ellen G. White, *The Great Controversy* (Mountain View, CA: Pacific Press, 1911), 482.

[193] Augustine. *The City of God*. Book XXI, Chapters 1–2.

a new destiny upon them.[194] John Calvin wrote that the final judgment is the moment when God "makes visible what has long been known to Him," exposing the genuine loyalty or rebellion present in every life.[195] Martin Luther emphasized that judgment vindicates God and reveals the authenticity of faith, showing whether a person trusted Christ or clung to self righteousness.[196] Their combined testimony echoes the biblical truth that God forces no one into salvation or destruction. The judgment unfolds before the universe so that every creature can see that God honors freedom and that human destiny is the result of human choice.

The judgment also unveils the fairness of God's dealings with humanity. J. N. Andrews wrote that the investigative judgment "vindicates the justice of God by presenting all the facts of each case before the universe."[197] Nothing is hidden. God invites examination, proving that His government is founded upon truth and love.

---

[194] Thomas Aquinas. *Summa Theologiae.* Supplement, Question 88, Article 1.

[195] John Calvin. *Institutes of the Christian Religion.* Book III, Chapter 25, Section 5.

[196] Martin Luther. *Lectures on Romans.* In *Luther's Works*, vol. 25.

[197] J. N. Andrews, *The Judgment: Its Events and Their Order* (Battle Creek, MI: Review and Herald, 1890), 15.

But the judgment also exposes the spiritual condition of those who live in the final generation. Scripture describes a church that believes itself rich, strong, and spiritually secure, yet is in reality "poor, wretched, pitiable, blind, and naked" (Revelation 3:17). Christ's counsel to Laodicea, "buy from Me gold refined in the fire… white garments… and eye salve" (Revelation 3:18), reveals that the greatest end time danger is not open rebellion but unconscious self-deception. The final judgment does not merely reveal God's fairness. It reveals our true need.

This condition parallels Jesus' parable of the ten virgins (Matthew 25:1-13). All ten had lamps. All ten had oil. All ten believed they were ready. Yet five discovered too late that their supply had run dry. Their failure was not the absence of belief but the absence of continual dependence on the Spirit. The investigative judgment exposes the difference between a profession of readiness and a life anchored in Christ. It is not designed to create fear but to awaken a sleeping church.

If the cross revealed Satan's defeat, the modern world reveals his desperation. Revelation warns that Satan attacks with "great wrath," knowing that "his time is short" (Revelation 12:12, ESV). Jesus Himself taught that the final generation would resemble the days of Noah and the days of Lot, when people were "eating and drinking, marrying and giving in marriage," and "buying and selling, planting and building" (Matthew 24:38; Luke 17:28, ESV). There is nothing sinful about these activities. The danger is that ordinary life becomes a distraction that blinds the heart to spiritual reality. Routine becomes anesthesia. Normalcy becomes deception. The enemy does not always destroy by force. He destroys by preoccupation. The digital world intensifies this condition, filling the mind with endless noise that drowns out the voice of God. The judgment therefore calls the believer back to clarity, vigilance, and dependence on Christ in a world designed to numb the conscience, divide attention, and lull the soul into complacency.

The judgment does not end with investigation. Scripture describes an executive phase when God renders final justice. Revelation states, "And the dead were judged by what was written in the books" (Revelation 20:12, ESV). This is not arbitrary sentencing. It is the recognition of free choices.

The destruction of the wicked is not an act of revenge. It is an act of mercy. The prophet Malachi writes, "The day that is coming shall set them ablaze" (Malachi 4:1, ESV). The Hebrew word שָׂרַף (saraph), meaning to consume or purify, illustrates that the fire does not torment eternally. It brings sin to an end.[198]

Ellen G. White affirms this truth with theological clarity: "The destruction of sin and sinners is an act of love."[199] To allow sin to continue would be to perpetuate misery. To eradicate sin is to restore peace.

Uriah Smith explains that "the final judgment is God's answer to rebellion and the securing of the universe against future apostasy."[200] Evil is not merely restricted. It is removed.

Satan himself faces judgment. Revelation declares, "The devil who had deceived them was thrown into the lake of fire" (Revelation 20:10, ESV). This act ends the long history of rebellion. The Greek verb κατεργάζομαι (katergazomai), used elsewhere to mean "bring to a full end," reflects the complete termination of Satan's influence.

Adventist scholar Norman Gulley writes that the final destruction of evil "preserves the moral coherence of the universe and guarantees that freedom will never

---

[198] HALOT, s.v. "פָּרַשׁ."

[199] Ellen G. White, *The Great Controversy*, 543.

[200] Uriah Smith, *Thoughts on Daniel and the Revelation* (Battle Creek, MI: Review and Herald, 1882), commentary on Daniel 7.

again be abused."[201] Once Satan and sin are eradicated, the entire creation stands in joyful security.

When sin is destroyed, God's people rejoice not because anyone perishes but because righteousness is restored. John writes, "He will wipe away every tear from their eyes" (Revelation 21:4, ESV). The eradication of sin is the foundation of eternal joy.

This chapter reveals that judgment is not the dark side of God. It is the radiant expression of His justice, mercy, and love. God does not destroy because He delights in punishment. He destroys because love demands the removal of suffering.

The great controversy ends not with confusion or fear, but with clarity. The universe understands. God's character is vindicated. His people are safe. Creation begins anew.

---

[201] Norman R. Gulley, *Systematic Theology: Eschatology* (Berrien Springs, MI: Andrews University Press, 2013), 261.

CHAPTER SEVENTEEN

The Eternal Restoration of All Things

As the final judgment reveals the justice of God's decisions, Chapter 17 lifts the reader to the ultimate moment of the controversy, when God Himself stands fully vindicated before the universe. The digital crisis of Chapter 15 exposes the enemy's desperation. The judgment of Chapter 16 exposes God's transparency. Now the closing of the controversy reveals something even greater: the full beauty of God's character. This is the moment toward which every chapter has been moving. The universe does not simply see that God has won. It sees why He is worthy of eternal trust.

The great controversy concludes with a restoration so complete and a revelation so compelling that the universe will never again question the goodness of God. When sin is gone, God's character stands fully vindicated. Every being, redeemed or unfallen, sees that His ways have always been just, loving, and true.

The climax of this vindication is expressed in Paul's cosmic vision:

"Every knee shall bow… and every tongue confess that Jesus Christ is Lord"

(Philippians 2:10 to 11, ESV). The Greek word ἐξομολογέω (exomologeō) means to openly acknowledge truth with full agreement. This confession is not coerced. It is freely given. Even Satan and the lost acknowledge that God has been righteous in all His ways.

The prophet Ezekiel says that when judgment is finished, "all nations shall know that I am the Lord" (Ezekiel 38:23, ESV). The Hebrew word עָדְי (yada), meaning to know intimately or acknowledge personally, shows this recognition is relational. The universe knows God not by force but by revelation.

Ellen White describes the scene with majestic simplicity: "As soon as the books of record are opened, and the eye of Jesus looks upon the wicked, they are conscious of every sin. Every mouth is stopped."[202] The silence of the wicked is not fear. It is understanding. Every false accusation collapses. Every deceptive claim evaporates. Every being recognizes that God has acted in perfect fairness.

James White wrote that the final vindication reveals that "the character of God shines brighter for having passed through the challenge of the ages."[203] The controversy does not weaken God's government. It eternally secures it.

---

[202] Ellen G. White, *The Great Controversy*, 666-667.
[203] James White, *Review and Herald*, April 9, 1861.

Creation itself rejoices in the restoration. John writes, "Behold, the dwelling place of God is with man" (Revelation 21:3, ESV). The Greek word σκηνόω (skēnoō), meaning to dwell or tabernacle, reveals intimacy. God is no longer hidden behind a veil, temple, or symbol. He lives among His people. Fellowship replaces separation. Joy replaces sorrow. Restoration replaces conflict.

The redeemed, safe forever, reflect the character of Christ. "They shall see His face" (Revelation 22:4, ESV). The Hebrew concept of "face" (סִּינָפ, panim) signifies presence, favor, and relationship. To see God's face means the removal of every barrier that sin ever introduced.

Gerhard Hasel writes that God's vindication is the "theological jewel at the center of eschatology."[204] Redemption is not merely the saving of humanity. It is the restoration of the universe. It is the eternal answer to the lie that began the controversy.

Ellen White describes the final vision: "One pulse of harmony and gladness beats through the vast creation."[205] This is not poetic exaggeration. It is the real

---

[204] Gerhard Hasel, "The Biblical Concept of Judgment," *Journal of the Adventist Theological Society* 2.1 (1991): 27.

[205] Ellen G. White, *The Great Controversy*, 678.

condition of a universe restored. Peace is not fragile. It is everlasting because it rests on understanding. God's love has been demonstrated to all. His character has been revealed beyond dispute.

The controversy ends because clarity ends confusion. Love ends rebellion. Truth ends deception.

The universe is secure.

God is vindicated.

And creation begins the eternal ages of joy in the presence of the One who has always been faithful.

Conclusion

The story of Lucifer's fall is more than a distant tale of cosmic rebellion. It is the foundation of the entire biblical narrative and the lens through which the moral drama of our world must be understood. Scripture presents Lucifer not as a symbol or an abstract metaphor, but as a real being whose character, intentions, and accusations are revealed with remarkable precision. The prophets describe his exalted position, the inward rise of pride, the corruption of his wisdom, and the slander he spread against the character and government of God. These are not guesses or theological assumptions. They arise directly from the biblical witness, and the Spirit of Prophecy, along with the careful work of Adventist pioneers, unfolds what Scripture has already declared.

When the prophets speak of Lucifer's beauty, wisdom, and anointed role, they reveal a being who began as a masterpiece of divine creation. His fall began in the heart, as the Hebrew word lev indicates. The heart in Scripture is the center of identity, intention, and moral direction. It was here that Lucifer turned inward. His heart was lifted up, and his wisdom was corrupted. This did not happen because of ignorance, deprivation, or outside pressure. It was a voluntary inward curve of the soul. Augustine later called this incurvatus in se, the moment when self becomes the center and the Creator becomes secondary. Scripture had already described this spiritual shift long before theologians named it.

Isaiah records Lucifer's ambition in five clear resolutions. I will ascend. I will exalt. I will sit. I will ascend. I will make myself like the Most High. These are not the words of a confused angel. They are the deliberate aims of a creature who sought a station that belongs only to God. Revelation confirms that this rebellion matured into open conflict. Jesus Himself testifies that He saw Satan fall like lightning from heaven. The biblical evidence leaves no uncertainty. Lucifer desired authority, worship, and rule. He desired what could never belong to a created being.

The controversy that began in heaven continued through every major scene of Scripture. The serpent in Eden questioned God's goodness. Satan accused Job and misrepresented the motives of God. The tempter confronted Christ in the wilderness. The dragon raged against the church. The last days present a crisis of worship in Revelation 13 and 14. His methods never change. Pride, deception, accusation, distortion of identity, and the reframing of God's character are his repeated strategies. The Adventist pioneers saw this thread clearly while studying Scripture. James White, Uriah Smith, J. N. Andrews, and others recognized that the entire biblical narrative displays this consistent pattern. Ellen White describes the relational and motivational dimensions, affirming that Lucifer's rebellion began with a misrepresentation of God's love and a claim that His law was restrictive and unfair. What she presents is not speculation. It is the logical and faithful reading of Scripture when all the linguistic, narrative, and theological evidence is brought together.

Today the great controversy enters its final scenes. The same lies that deceived angels now saturate the modern world. The inward curve of pride, once born in Lucifer's heart, has become a celebrated virtue. A world shaped by image, performance, comparison, and self display reflects the spirit of the one who first sought to ascend and exalt himself. Technology itself is not evil, but the spirit of self worship finds a fertile environment in digital culture. Humanity has embraced ways of thinking that reflect the fallen cherub more than the humble Christ.

Today the controversy often unfolds in quieter ways. Satan rarely approaches with open defiance. Instead he works through distraction, self-absorption, digital noise, and the endless pull of comparison. What began in Lucifer's heart now appears in a world shaped by image, performance, and curated identity. The battlefield of the final generation is not simply doctrinal. It is attentional. It is the struggle to keep the mind fixed on Christ in a culture designed to fracture focus and turn the heart inward. The same inward curve that corrupted the highest angel now threatens to shape modern humanity. This is why the final call of Scripture urges clarity, sobriety, and devotion in an age of unprecedented distraction.

Yet the great controversy is not ultimately about Lucifer. It is about God. It is about the truth of His character and the beauty of His love. Lucifer misrepresented the Creator. Christ revealed Him. Lucifer exalted himself. Christ emptied Himself. Lucifer grasped for a throne. Christ chose a cross. Lucifer rejected divine love. Christ embodied it. From heaven to Eden, from the wilderness to the cross, from the resurrection to the final judgment, Christ responds to every accusation not with force, but with truth. He uses no coercion. He overcomes through self giving love.

When the controversy comes to its end, the universe will not only acknowledge the power of God. It will testify to His goodness. The redeemed and the lost will confess the justice and mercy of God, not because they are forced, but because the evidence is undeniable. The defeat of Satan becomes the vindication of God.

Scripture has revealed who Lucifer was, why he fell, what he became, and how he works. Adventist theology, grounded in Scripture and enriched by the Spirit of Prophecy, has traced this conflict from beginning to end. As the final scenes unfold, the call to every believer is unmistakable. Reject the inward curve of pride. Embrace the outward facing love of Christ. Resist the deception of a world that mirrors Lucifer's character. Stand with the One who humbled Himself to save us. Fear God. Give Him glory. Worship Him who created the heavens and the earth (Revelation 14:7).

The rebellion began with a creature grasping for divinity. It ends with humanity restored to God through the humility of Christ. In this cosmic drama every life becomes a testimony, and every choice becomes a declaration. The universe watches as the story reaches its conclusion, and the people of God are invited to stand with the Lamb who gave everything so that creation could once again shine with the light Lucifer once reflected and ultimately rejected.

Bibliography

Books, Commentaries, Monographs

Andrews, J. N. The Judgment: Its Events and Their Order. Battle Creek, MI: Review and Herald, 1890.

—————. The Sanctuary and the Twenty-Three Hundred Days. Battle Creek, MI: Review and Herald, 1872.

—————. The Thoughts of God Toward Man. Battle Creek, MI: Review and Herald, 1865.

Athanasius. On the Incarnation. Translated by John Behr. Yonkers, NY: St. Vladimir's Seminary Press, 2011.

Augustine. City of God. Translated by Henry Bettenson. London: Penguin, 2003.

—————. Confessions. Translated by Henry Chadwick. Oxford: Oxford University Press, 1991.

—————. On the Trinity. Translated by Edmund Hill. Brooklyn, NY: New City Press, 1991.

—————. Tractates on the Gospel of John. Translated by John Gibb. Edinburgh: T&T Clark, 1888.

Bauckham, Richard. Jesus and the God of Israel. Grand Rapids, MI: Eerdmans, 2008.

————. The Climax of Prophecy. Edinburgh: T&T Clark, 1993.

Beale, G. K. A New Testament Biblical Theology. Grand Rapids, MI: Baker Academic, 2011.

Block, Daniel I. The Book of Ezekiel, Chapters 25–48. Grand Rapids, MI: Eerdmans, 1998.

Bruce, F. F. The Epistle to the Hebrews. Grand Rapids, MI: Eerdmans, 1990.

Calvin, John. Institutes of the Christian Religion. Translated by Henry Beveridge. Peabody, MA: Hendrickson, 2008.

————. Commentary on the First Epistle to the Corinthians. Translated by John Pringle. Grand Rapids, MI: Baker, 2003.

————. Commentary on Job. Translated by Joseph Haroutunian. Grand Rapids, MI: Eerdmans, 1952.

Delitzsch, Franz, and C. F. Keil. Commentary on the Old Testament. Vol. 9. Peabody, MA: Hendrickson, 1989.

Ellul, Jacques. The Technological Society. New York: Vintage Books, 1964.

France, R. T. The Gospel of Matthew. Grand Rapids, MI: Eerdmans, 2007.

Gane, Roy. *Leviticus, Numbers*. Grand Rapids, MI: Zondervan, 2004.

Gulley, Norman R. *Systematic Theology: Prolegomena*. Berrien Springs, MI: Andrews University Press, 2003.

———. *Systematic Theology: Eschatology*. Berrien Springs, MI: Andrews University Press, 2013.

Hasel, Gerhard. *Old Testament Theology: Basic Issues in the Current Debate*. Grand Rapids, MI: Eerdmans, 1991.

———. *The Remnant: The History and Theology of the Remnant Idea*. Berrien Springs, MI: Andrews University Press, 1974.

Haskell, Stephen N. *The Story of the Seer of Patmos*. South Lancaster, MA: Bible Training School, 1905.

Keener, Craig S. *The Gospel of Matthew: A Socio-Rhetorical Commentary*. Grand Rapids, MI: Eerdmans, 2009.

———. *The Gospel of Mark: A Socio-Rhetorical Commentary*. Grand Rapids, MI: Eerdmans, 2019.

Ladd, George Eldon. *A Theology of the New Testament*. Grand Rapids, MI: Eerdmans, 1993.

Longman III, Tremper, and John H. Walton. The Lost World of Adam and Eve. Downers Grove, IL: InterVarsity Press, 2015.

Luther, Martin. Lectures on Genesis, Chapters 1–5. Vol. 1 of Luther's Works. Edited by Jaroslav Pelikan. St. Louis, MO: Concordia, 1958.

———. Lectures on Genesis, Chapters 6–14. Vol. 2. St. Louis, MO: Concordia, 1960.

———. Lectures on Job. Vol. 54. St. Louis, MO: Concordia, 1967.

———. Lectures on Romans. Vol. 25. St. Louis, MO: Concordia, 1972.

McGrath, Alister. The Twilight of Atheism. New York: Doubleday, 2004.

Milton, John. Paradise Lost. In The Complete Poetry and Essential Prose of John Milton, edited by William Kerrigan, John Rumrich, and Stephen Fallon. New York: Modern Library, 2007.

Oswalt, John N. The Book of Isaiah, Chapters 1–39. Grand Rapids, MI: Eerdmans, 1986.

Paulien, Jon. What the Bible Says About the End-Time. Hagerstown, MD: Review and Herald, 1994.

Postman, Neil. Amusing Ourselves to Death. New York: Penguin, 1985.

von Rad, Gerhard. Wisdom in Israel. Nashville, TN: Abingdon Press, 1972.

Waggoner, E. J. Christ and His Righteousness. Oakland, CA: Pacific Press, 1890.

Walton, John H. The Lost World of Adam and Eve. Downers Grove, IL: InterVarsity Press, 2015.

White, Ellen G. The Desire of Ages. Mountain View, CA: Pacific Press, 1898.

—————. The Great Controversy. Mountain View, CA: Pacific Press, 1911.

—————. Mind, Character, and Personality. Vol. 1. Nashville, TN: Southern Publishing, 1977.

—————. Patriarchs and Prophets. Oakland, CA: Pacific Press, 1890.

—————. Steps to Christ. Mountain View, CA: Pacific Press, 1892.

—————. The Story of Redemption. Washington, DC: Review and Herald, 1947.

White, James. Gospel Works. Battle Creek, MI: Review and Herald, 1870.

———. Life Incidents in Connection with the Great Advent Movement. Battle Creek, MI: Steam Press, 1868.

———. The Law and the Gospel. Battle Creek, MI: Review and Herald, 1870.

Journal & Periodical Articles

Andrews, J. N. "The Origin of Evil." Review and Herald, January 14, 1873.

———. Various writings in Review and Herald, including February 7, 1856.

Hasel, Gerhard. "The Biblical Concept of Judgment." Journal of the Adventist Theological Society 2.1 (1991): 27–37.

———. "The Cosmic Controversy Theme in Scripture." Journal of the Adventist Theological Society 5.1 (1994): 27–31.

———. "The Love of God and the Law of God." Journal of the Adventist Theological Society 2.1 (1991): 13–18.

Paulien, Jon. "The Cosmic Conflict." Adventist Review, October 2004.

Paulien, Jon. "The Great Controversy Theme." Adventist Review, 2004.

Rodríguez, Ángel Manuel. "The Origin of Evil." Adventist Review, July 2007.

———. "The Vindication of God." Biblical Research Institute, 2005.

———. "Lessons from the Story of Job." Adventist Review, March 2010.

Smith, Uriah. Articles in Review and Herald, including coverage on Revelation 12 (multiple years).

White, James. Review and Herald: January 9, 1855; January 28, 1858; April 9, 1861; June 9, 1857.

White, James, ed. The Signs of the Times, March 12, 1874.

Modern Academic Journal Articles

Nesi, Jessica. "Using Social Media for Social Comparison and Feedback Seeking." Journal of Abnormal Child Psychology 43 (2015): 405–417.

Samra, Aisha, et al. "Social Comparisons: A Potential Mechanism Linking Problematic Social Media Use with Depression." Frontiers in Psychology 13 (2022): 1–12.

U.S. Department of Health & Human Services. Social Media and Youth Mental Health: The U.S. Surgeon General's Advisory. Washington, DC: HHS, 2023.

Reference Works & Lexicons

BDAG — Danker, Frederick William, ed. A Greek–English Lexicon of the New Testament and Other Early Christian Literature. 3rd ed. Chicago: University of Chicago Press, 2000.

BDB — Brown, Francis, S. R. Driver, and Charles A. Briggs. The Brown-Driver-Briggs Hebrew and English Lexicon. Peabody, MA: Hendrickson, 1996.

HALOT — Koehler, Ludwig, Walter Baumgartner, and Johann Jakob Stamm. The Hebrew and Aramaic Lexicon of the Old Testament. Leiden: Brill, 1994–2000.

Appendix A:
Hebrew Word Studies

Introduction

This appendix gathers the primary Hebrew terms foundational to the study of Lucifer's character and motives. These words appear throughout the biblical narrative and form the linguistic core of the Great Controversy theme. Each entry reflects how Scripture describes the inward turning of Lucifer's heart, the rise of pride, and the corruption of wisdom.

Key Hebrew Terms

בֵּל (lev): [206] The inner self, the seat of thought, identity, and will. Ezekiel uses this term to show the internal nature of Lucifer's pride.

סוּר / הבג (gabah / rum): [207] To be high, lifted up. Used to describe Lucifer's self exaltation and inward rise of pride.

---

[206] Francis Brown, S. R. Driver, and Charles A. Briggs, *The Brown Driver Briggs Hebrew and English Lexicon* (Peabody, MA: Hendrickson, 1996), s.v. "בֵל."

[207] Brown, Driver, and Briggs, *Hebrew and English Lexicon*, s.v. "הבג"; Daniel I. Block, *The Book of Ezekiel, Chapters 25–48* (Grand Rapids, MI: Eerdmans, 1998), 94.

תחש (shichat): [208] To corrupt, ruin, or twist. Ezekiel applies this verb to Lucifer's wisdom, showing distortion rather than loss.

המד (damah): [209] To resemble or be like. Isaiah uses this to capture Lucifer's ambition to make himself like the Most High.

הָלְכְּר (rekullah): [210] Slanderous tale bearing. Describes how Lucifer spread accusations and misrepresentations among the angels.

סוּרָע (arum): [211] Crafty or subtle. A term used for the serpent in Eden, reflecting calculated deception.

בּוּרְכ (keruv): [212] A high angelic being associated with God's throne and presence. Ezekiel uses this term for Lucifer's original role as the anointed guardian cherub.

---

[208] Brown, Driver, and Briggs, *Hebrew and English Lexicon*, s.v. "תחש."

[209] Brown, Driver, and Briggs, *Hebrew and English Lexicon*, s.v. "המד."

[210] Brown, Driver, and Briggs, *Hebrew and English Lexicon*, s.v. "הָלְכְּר"; C. F. Keil and F. Delitzsch, *Commentary on the Old Testament*, vol. 9 (Peabody, MA: Hendrickson, 1989), 340.

[211] Brown, Driver, and Briggs, *Hebrew and English Lexicon*, s.v. "סוּרָע."

[212] Brown, Driver, and Briggs, Hebrew and English Lexicon, s.v. "בּוּרְכ."

הָרֹת (torah):[213] Instruction or law. Central to Lucifer's attacks on God's government and character.

סֹת (tom):[214] Completeness or integrity. Ezekiel applies this to Lucifer to describe his original moral wholeness before iniquity arose.

---

[213] Brown, Driver, and Briggs, *Hebrew and English Lexicon*, s.v. "הָרֹת."
[214] Brown, Driver, and Briggs, Hebrew and English Lexicon, s.v. "סֹת."

Appendix B:
Greek Word Studies

Introduction

This appendix organizes the key Greek terms used throughout the New Testament to describe Satan's nature, actions, and ongoing work in the world. These words strengthen the biblical picture of deception, accusation, and rebellion.

Key Greek Terms

διάβολος (diabolos): [215] Slanderer, accuser. Reveals Satan's identity as one who divides through false charges.

κατήγορος (kategoros): [216] Accuser in legal language. The title used in Revelation for Satan's continual accusations.

πλανάω (planao): [217] To lead astray. Describes Satan's active work in deceiving the whole world.

---

[215] Frederick William Danker, ed., *A Greek English Lexicon of the New Testament and Other Early Christian Literature*, 3rd ed. (Chicago: University of Chicago Press, 2000), s.v. "διάβολος."

[216] Danker, *Greek English Lexicon*, s.v. "κατήγορος."

[217] Danker, *Greek English Lexicon*, s.v. "πλανάω."

ψεύστης (pseustes): [218] Liar. Jesus calls Satan the father of lies in John 8:44.

πόλεμος (polemos): [219] War or conflict. Used to describe the cosmic struggle in Revelation 12.

πειράζω (peirazo): [220] To test or tempt. Used in the temptation narrative to reveal Satan's strategies.

τετέλεσται (tetelestai): [221] It is finished. Christ's declaration of victory over Satan at the cross.

δειγματίζω (deigmatizo): [222] To expose or make a public example. Used to describe Christ's triumph over the powers of darkness.

ἐξομολογέω (exomologeo): [223] To confess or acknowledge. Linked to the final acknowledgment of God's justice.

---

[218] Danker, *Greek English Lexicon*, s.v. "ψεύστης."

[219] Danker, *Greek English Lexicon*, s.v. "πόλεμος."

[220] Danker, *Greek English Lexicon*, s.v. "πειράζω."

[221] Danker, *Greek English Lexicon*, s.v. "τετέλεσται."

[222] Danker, *Greek English Lexicon*, s.v. "δειγματίζω."

[223] Danker, *Greek English Lexicon*, s.v. "ἐξομολογέω."

Appendix C:
Pioneer Quotes

Pioneer Quotations on Lucifer, Rebellion, and the Government of God

The early Adventist pioneers approached the subject of Lucifer with careful study and a deep respect for the biblical narrative. Their writings demonstrate that the Adventist understanding of the Great Controversy is rooted in Scripture itself. The quotations collected here reflect how they understood Lucifer's position, pride, accusations, rebellion, and final defeat.

Lucifer's Original Position

"The most exalted position in heaven next to Christ."[224]

"Ruled in justice, yet His authority was the expression of benevolence."[225]

The Rise of Pride and the Corruption of Wisdom

---

[224] James White, Life Incidents in Connection with the Great Advent Movement (Battle Creek, MI: Steam Press, 1868), 295.

[225] James White, ed., The Signs of the Times, March 12, 1874, 1.

"When he permitted the admiration of himself to eclipse his admiration of the character of God."[226]

"Pride perverted his wisdom and corrupted his loyalty."[227]

"A blind ambition to occupy the place of Christ."[228]

Accusations, Misrepresentations, and Slander

"Angels needed no law to govern them."

"A misapprehension of God's goodness."[229]

"Claimed a place which pertained not to him but to Christ alone."[230]

The War in Heaven

"The war in heaven was the inevitable result of Satan's persistence in rebellion."[231]

---

[226] James White, Life Incidents in Connection with the Great Advent Movement (Battle Creek, MI: Steam Press, 1868), 295.

[227] J. N. Andrews, "The Origin of Evil," Review and Herald, January 14, 1873, 52.

[228] J. N. Andrews, The Sanctuary and the Twenty Three Hundred Days (Battle Creek, MI: Review and Herald, 1872), 132.

[229] Uriah Smith, Thoughts on Daniel and the Revelation (Battle Creek, MI: Review and Herald, 1897), 430.

[230] Uriah Smith, Thoughts on Daniel and the Revelation (Battle Creek, MI: Review and Herald, 1897), 431.

[231] James White, Review and Herald, June 9, 1857.

"The first sorrow heaven ever knew was when Lucifer and his followers were cast out."[232]

"Still cherished hopes of ultimately succeeding."[233]

Lucifer After the Fall

"Allowed his envy of Christ to prevail, and he became rebellious."[234]

"Deprived of his position, all the heavenly host acknowledged the justice of God."[235]

"Saw that his disguise was torn away."[236]

Satan's Work on Earth

"The Son of God and the prince of heaven, His equal, came into conflict."[237]

---

[232] Stephen N. Haskell, The Story of the Seer of Patmos (South Lancaster, MA: Bible Training School, 1905), 27.

[233] Uriah Smith, Daniel and the Revelation (Battle Creek, MI: Review and Herald, 1897), 431.

[234] Ellen G. White, Patriarchs and Prophets (Oakland, CA: Pacific Press, 1890), 35.

[235] Ellen G. White, The Great Controversy (Mountain View, CA: Pacific Press, 1911), 495.

[236] Ellen G. White, The Great Controversy (Mountain View, CA: Pacific Press, 1911), 493.

[237] Ellen G. White, The Desire of Ages (Oakland, CA: Pacific Press, 1898), 114.

"The allegiance of His creatures must rest upon a conviction of His justice and benevolence."[238]

<hr>

[238] Ellen G. White, The Story of Redemption (Washington, DC: Review and Herald, 1947), 424.

Appendix D: Glossary of Key Terms

This glossary provides brief and accessible definitions of the major biblical, theological, linguistic, and Adventist terms used throughout this book. These explanations are written for readers who may not have formal training in Hebrew, Greek, or systematic theology, yet desire to understand the concepts at the heart of the Great Controversy theme.

Adversary

A biblical title for Satan referring to one who opposes, resists, and attempts to obstruct the work of God. Appears in Job 1 and Zechariah 3.

Accuser

A title used for Satan in Revelation 12. It describes his work in bringing accusations against God and His people. Connected to the Greek term kategoros.

Anointed Cherub

A title from Ezekiel 28 describing Lucifer's exalted position in heaven. Indicates nearness to God's throne and a role of high trust and authority.

Character of God

The consistent theme that God is love, just, faithful, merciful, and transparent in all His ways. The Great Controversy revolves around Satan's misrepresentations of God's character.

Corruption of Wisdom

A phrase drawn from Ezekiel 28 describing how Lucifer distorted his God given wisdom by turning it inward toward self exaltation.

Cosmic Conflict

Another expression for the Great Controversy. Describes the universal struggle between Christ and Satan, centered on truth, freedom, loyalty, and worship.

Deception

A key aspect of Satan's work. The Greek term planao describes deliberate distortion of truth. Satan uses misrepresentation to turn minds away from God.

Elohim

A Hebrew word for God that appears throughout the Old Testament. It expresses His power, majesty, and sovereign authority.

Exaltation

The act of lifting oneself above the place God assigned. Lucifer's exaltation is described through Hebrew terms like gabah and rum.

Great Controversy

The overarching biblical narrative of conflict between God and Satan that spans heaven, earth, and the final restoration. Central to Adventist theology.

Holiness

The purity, moral perfection, and complete righteousness of God. Lucifer's rebellion began in the presence of divine holiness.

Incurvatus in se

A theological expression meaning "turned inward on oneself." Describes how Lucifer bent his affections away from God toward self admiration.

Judgment

The process by which God reveals truth, vindicates His people, and exposes the claims of Satan. Always rooted in justice and mercy.

Law of God

God's moral character expressed through His commandments. Satan's accusations often targeted the fairness, necessity, or goodness of God's law.

Lev

Hebrew word for heart. Refers not to emotion but to the inner person, including thought, identity, and will. Used in Scripture to describe the root of Lucifer's pride.

Michael

A title for Christ in His role as Commander of the heavenly host. Seen in Daniel 12 and Revelation 12. Represents divine authority against Satan.

Pride

The beginning of Lucifer's fall. Pride is the elevation of self above God and others. The biblical root of all rebellion.

Rebellion

The intentional breaking of trust and refusal to submit to God's authority. Lucifer's rebellion began internally and spread through slander.

Rekullah

A Hebrew term meaning secret tale bearing or slanderous trading. Ezekiel uses this word to describe Lucifer's circulation of accusations in heaven.

Satan

Means "adversary." Refers to Lucifer after his fall. Describes his role in opposing God's character, law, and people.

Self-Exaltation

The core of Lucifer's sin. Seen in his desire to raise his throne above the stars of God and to make himself like the Most High.

Torah

Hebrew for instruction or law. More than legal regulation, it expresses God's teaching and guidance. Central to Satan's accusations in heaven and Eden.

War in Heaven

Described in Revelation 12. Not a physical war but a conflict of truth and deception. Michael and His angels fought against the dragon.

Wisdom

In Scripture, a combination of knowledge, discernment, and moral understanding. Lucifer corrupted his wisdom by turning it toward self serving ambition.

Worship

The highest expression of loyalty and allegiance. The final conflict centers on worship, either of the Creator or of the self exalted power.

Appendix E:
Timeline of the Great Controversy

Introduction

This timeline presents the major movements of the Great Controversy from its earliest stages in heaven to its final resolution in the new earth. It is not intended to be exhaustive but to guide the reader through the flow of biblical history as it unfolds the character of God and the rebellion of Satan.

1. The Creation of Lucifer

God creates an exalted, glorious being described as perfect in wisdom and beauty (Ezekiel 28:12–15). Lucifer stands nearest the throne and holds a position of high trust.

2. The First Rise of Pride

Lucifer turns his thoughts inward. His heart becomes lifted up because of his beauty (Ezekiel 28:17). This marks the beginning of sin in the universe.

3. Whispered Discontent and Slander

Lucifer circulates dissatisfaction among the angels. Ezekiel describes this with the imagery of secret trading or tale bearing (Ezekiel 28:16). He misrepresents God's character and stirs doubt.

4. The Open Challenge to Christ

Lucifer contests the authority of the Son of God and seeks equality with Him (Isaiah 14:13–14). This becomes a direct challenge to the government of heaven.

5. War in Heaven

A decisive conflict breaks out. Michael and His angels fight against the dragon and his angels (Revelation 12:7). This war is a conflict of truth versus deception, not physical weapons.

6. The Casting Out of Satan

Satan and his followers are expelled from heaven (Revelation 12:9).

Jesus later testifies, "I saw Satan fall like lightning from heaven" (Luke 10:18).

7. The Fall of Humanity

Satan deceives Eve in Eden using misrepresentation and doubt (Genesis 3:1–5).

Sin enters the human experience.

8. The Conflict Expands Through Earth's History

Job, the patriarchs, Israel, the prophets, and the kings all experience the effects of the controversy (Job 1; Daniel 10). Heaven continues observing the unfolding struggle (1 Corinthians 4:9).

9. The Temptation and Ministry of Jesus

Satan attacks Christ directly in the wilderness temptations (Matthew 4:1–11).

Christ reveals the true character of God and exposes the deceiver.

10. The Cross and Supreme Victory

Jesus declares "It is finished" (John 19:30). Colossians 2:15 states that Christ disarmed the principalities and powers and made a public example of them.

11. The Last-Day Deceptions

Revelation describes a global conflict over worship, truth, loyalty, and identity (Revelation 13 and 14). Satan intensifies deception as the end draws near.

12. The Millennium and Final Judgment

Satan is bound for a thousand years while the redeemed review God's judgments (Revelation 20:1–3). Afterward he is released briefly and then destroyed.

13. The Destruction of Satan and Sin

Satan is cast into the lake of fire and becomes ashes (Ezekiel 28:19; Revelation 20:10).

Evil is permanently eradicated.

14. The Restoration of All Things

God creates a new heaven and a new earth where righteousness dwells (Revelation 21–22). The universe is at peace and God's character is fully vindicated.

Appendix F:
Scripture Index

OLD TESTAMENT

Genesis
3:5 — 15, 26, 37, 58

Isaiah
14:13–14 — 8
30:18 — 41
65:17 — 43

Ezekiel
28:14 — 4
28:16 — 8
28:17 — 7, 24

Daniel
7:9 — 41
7:10 — 41
10:21 — 19
12:1 — 19

Malachi
4:1 — 42

NEW TESTAMENT

Matthew
4:4 — 56
4:5–6 — 56
4:9–10 — 56

John
1:1 — 19
12:31 — 56
19:30 — 56

Colossians
1:19 — 19

1 Timothy
3:6 — 8

2 Timothy
3:2–5 — 37

Philippians
2:10–11 — 43

Revelation

Appendix G:
Digital Identity and the Great Controversy

A Contemporary Application of the Cosmic Conflict

Introduction

The Great Controversy is not confined to ancient history. The same principles that animated Lucifer's rebellion are active in modern society. Today, one of Satan's most effective tools is the digital environment that shapes identity, attention, relationships, and self-worth. Technology itself is not evil, but the enemy uses it to distort the image of God in humanity.

1. The Original Lie Repackaged for the Digital Age

In Eden, the serpent declared, "You will be like God" (Genesis 3:5).

The temptation was not merely curiosity. It was identity distortion.

Today, digital culture echoes the same message:

- Create your own image
- Define your own truth
- Exalt yourself
- Seek admiration
- Craft perfection
- Live for validation

This is not neutral. It mirrors Lucifer's own ambition recorded in Isaiah 14:13–14.

2. Distraction as a Spiritual Strategy

Satan's most effective modern weapon is not violence but distraction.

Distraction erodes spiritual awareness.

It breaks the connection between the human heart and the presence of God.

Digital platforms are designed to:

- hold attention
- fragment focus
- overload the mind
- numb the conscience

The controversy over worship in Revelation is ultimately a controversy over attention.

3. Comparison, Envy, and Self-Exaltation

Social media conditions people to measure worth by:

- appearance
- achievements
- likes
- followers
- digital applause

This fosters:

- envy
- insecurity
- pride
- competition

These are the same internal distortions that led to Lucifer's fall.

4. Curated Identity and Loss of Authenticity

Younger generations increasingly build identities online.

Curated identity creates:

- emotional instability
- addiction to approval
- fractured self-understanding

- distance from real spiritual life

This is the modern expression of Satan's work in Eden:

"You will be like God" becomes

"Create your own identity apart from God."

5. The Form of Godliness Without Power

Second Timothy 3 describes the last days:

- lovers of self
- lovers of pleasure
- proud
- without self-control
- having the appearance of godliness

This describes modern digital spirituality:

- inspirational quotes
- superficial religion
- selective morality
- performance-driven piety

A spirituality without surrender.

A faith without transformation.

6. The Final Battle for the Mind

The Great Controversy culminates in a conflict over worship and loyalty.

Revelation describes a contest over:

- truth
- identity
- allegiance
- character

The mind becomes the battlefield.

Digital identity becomes one of Satan's last tools for shaping loyalty.

Conclusion

Technology is not the enemy.

The real danger is a digital environment shaped by the same motives that once corrupted Lucifer's heart.

The call of Christ in the last days is a call back to:

- authentic identity
- true worship
- undivided mind
- wholehearted love
- spiritual clarity

The controversy ends when the image of God is restored in His people and every created being acknowledges the justice, goodness, and love of the Creator.